To Samwise

All the Best

Beverly ☺

Come fly with me

Come

BEVERLY DELICH

with SHELLEY FRALIC

fly with me

MICHAEL BUBLÉ'S
RISE TO STARDOM

((*a memoir*))

Douglas & McIntyre

Douglas and McIntyre (2013) Ltd.
P.O. Box 219, Madeira Park, BC V0N 2H0
www.douglas-mcintyre.com

Cataloguing data available from Library and Archives Canada
ISBN 978-1-77162-006-2 (cloth)
ISBN 978-1-77162-007-9 (ebook)

Edited by Shirarose Wilensky
Index by Stephen Ullstrom
Cover design by Carleton Wilson and Anna Comfort O'Keeffe
Text design by Mary White
Cover photos: Top inset, Michael Bublé 1996, David Clark photo/
The Province. Centre inset: Beverley Delich and Michael Bublé, Ann
Hamilton photo/*North Shore News*. Background image: Thinkstock.
Printed and bound in Canada

We gratefully acknowledge the financial support of the Canada
Council for the Arts, the British Columbia Arts Council, the Province
of British Columbia through the Book Publishing Tax Credit and
the Government of Canada through the Canada Book Fund for our
publishing activities.

Contents

Acknowledgements

Everyone has a story to tell, a tale of challenge and hardship, of joy and sorrow, of triumph and tragedy. What, then, compels some to write their memoirs, to be driven to share their personal lives in such a public way, while others wouldn't dream of stepping outside the boundaries of privacy?

It may be as simple as a need to reflect, and share. For many, the autobiography is cathartic, a letting go of secrets. For others, it's an opportunity to educate, or perhaps entertain. Sometimes, it's just a good story that seems worth telling.

For me, it's all of the above.

Mine has a been a life of twists and turns, of transformation and self-discovery, the varied textures of my seventy-plus years having been inexorably woven into the strong, lush fabric of a life well-lived. From a hardscrabble childhood in Montana marked by parental constraint to an adulthood of unbridled social freedom, from my marriage to my children to my various careers, the roller coaster of highs and lows has been both ordinary and extraordinary.

And it was never more so than in 1993, when at the age of fifty-three I crossed paths with a promising young singer from Burnaby and, within a few years, embarked with him upon one of the most unlikely and exhilarating adventures we could ever imagine.

This book could not have been written without the people who have always been in my corner, the friends and family who have been with me every step of the way.

Gratitude, for them and so much more, is in order.

To my family—my son, Daniel, and his wife, Kelly; my daughter, Lisa, and her husband, Mike; my wonderful grandchildren, Taylor and Mikayla; and my sister, Jerri, and brother, Robert—for their love and spirit and never-ending support.

To Michael Bublé, for starring in my life's second act.

To Shelley Fralic, for helping me put it all into words.

Come Fly with Me is my story, told with heart and with truth.

—BEVERLY DELICH

Come Fly with Me

The plane lifted off, circled above the whitecaps of the Pacific and levelled out in the clouds over the mountains of Washington State as it headed south, Vancouver International Airport a shrinking speck behind us, Nevada on the horizon ahead.

It was September 27, 2001, a bright, clear Thursday morning, and we were less than three hours away from landing at McCarran International in Las Vegas, where fortune can be found in a slot machine and where our future was waiting, the future we'd been working toward for eight long years.

This flight, on Alaska Airlines, felt more secure than any flight Michael and I had been on before. Security had been tight out of YVR, heralding a new age of nervousness on the ground and in the air that would take hold throughout the world and not let go, the horror of planes imploding those twin towers on the New York skyline still so fresh in the mind and heavy in the heart.

But I felt no fear as we settled into our seats, only an odd lightness, for ahead lay promise. This flight, I just knew, was different, nothing like those trips we had taken in past years, to places like Memphis and Toronto, trips so often marked by hope and then disappointment, so often about scrambling to survive while success, waiting in the wings, mocked us with its elusiveness.

But this flight, this was the one that would change everything. I could feel it in my bones.

Michael and I were booked into the MGM Grand Hotel, at the invitation of powerhouse music producer David Foster, who had arranged for Michael to be the opening act for comic and *Tonight Show* host Jay Leno.

Jay Leno. I could hardly believe it.

Jay, sensing that his fellow Americans were spooked by the unsettling terrorist threat of September 11, was giving free tickets to two of his performances at the MGM Grand theater for anyone courageous enough to fly into Las Vegas for the weekend. This was his way to prove to the fly-shy that the most powerful nation on earth needed to get back to business.

Jay wanted a singer to open his show, and that singer was to be Michael. My Michael. Michael Bublé, who had so impressed David, when he sang a year before at the wedding of former Canadian prime minister Brian Mulroney's daughter, that David had been booking him ever since for various events around the country. David had convinced his friend Jay that this young Canadian singing sensation was the perfect first act, the ideal antidote to lift the mood of a shell-shocked audience looking for diversion, if only for an hour or two, from the tragedy that had so levelled their spirit.

But up in the sky, as the jet cruised south and the Vegas revellers in the seats around us began their party planning, all I could think about was how surreal it was that after years of struggling for recognition, after all the talent shows and travelling revues and endless auditions and heart-rending rejections and false starts, with nothing but hope in our pockets and talent on our resume, this might be our time.

Michael sat directly across the aisle from me, where he always did when we flew, so that we could talk and still have private time, as well as leg room, and I knew that we must have made an unlikely pair, me the sixty-one-year-old manager and confidante, he the charismatic, impish twenty-six-year-old protege.

"Should I tell them, or do you want to?" Michael said, leaning toward me and motioning to his seatmates, who turned out to be two disc jockeys from the Rock 101 radio station back home in Vancouver. Bro Jake and Ollie had recognized Michael from the many shows he had done in the Vancouver area and were wondering aloud what we were up to in Las Vegas, what our relationship was, who I was.

"You tell him," I said to Michael.

I could only smile at how it must look and how no one, really, would believe it and how I intuitively knew that we were flying headlong into a new beginning.

CHAPTER ONE

I Was Made for Music

*M*y mother didn't want me to leave. I knew that. Not only would she miss me, in her own way, but I knew she would have trouble giving up the tight control that she'd always had on me, on everything I did, an unwavering stranglehold ever since I could remember, from the time I was a little girl and couldn't have friends and all the way through my high school years, when I wasn't allowed to date or socialize with anyone.

And even now. Even though I was twenty-four. A grown woman.

But I needed to be free. I had seldom been on a field trip, or attended school events outside of school hours. There had been no sleepovers or picnics for me, none of the fun things that a girl growing up in Butte, Montana, in the 1940s might do with her friends, none of the things that young people in bustling mining towns all over small-town America were doing.

It was a suffocating way to grow up, for I was innately

social and loved meeting people and going on adventures and dressing up. I loved music and singing and dancing and wanted more than anything to have friends over to my house, so many friends that I could spend entire weekends playing with them and going to their houses to meet their moms and dads and brothers and sisters.

So when I decided that I'd had enough and was moving out, that I could no longer chafe against her maternal restraints, it was a shock to her. How could this daughter of hers, this girl who had always done what she was told, just up and leave, just like that? It was the ultimate betrayal, at least for my mother, and was something a proper young lady did not do.

But I knew I had to.

It was 1964, and my world was coming alive. I had been an attentive student and did my best to be a good and obedient daughter. I got a job in my teens, and even while handing over my paycheques to Ma, which is what my siblings and I always called her, I had been thinking about leaving home, almost from the time I graduated from high school.

So I began looking for a place to live on my own. A little apartment was all I needed, and when I found it, I couldn't believe my luck. It was in downtown Butte, close to my job at the Montana Telephone Company but not too close to the little house I shared with Ma and my older brother, Robert, and little sister, Jerri.

It was small and not much, but it was mine. And it meant freedom. For the first time in my life, I could do what I wanted, when I wanted. I could come and go as I pleased, and talk to whomever I felt like talking to, and go out for dinner and meet my friends from work and go dancing until late.

But my decision to leave was a slap in the face to my mother, Josephine. Years later, imbued with the wisdom and perspective that age affords us, I came to understand that she had her own reasons for raising us with so little compassion, her own reasons for being so strict with us, and I knew that it had much to do with her own unhappy childhood in Serbia in the early 1900s. That hardscrabble life couldn't have been easy for her, and it didn't get much better when Josephine and her family—she had five siblings and was the second oldest of four girls—moved to Montana when she was only two. Life on American soil was chaotic and rough. A sister died, a brother married and moved to California and times were tough for the immigrant family.

Ma never talked much about those days, except for a story she would often tell about the day when she was fourteen and rushed home from her last day of Grade 8 to be greeted at the door by her mother and father, who ushered her into the family parlour. Waiting for her was a thirty-three-year-old man her parents had arranged for her to marry. She was told to say yes, and three days later, she was a bride moving to the tiny town of Tonopah, Nevada.

Her husband was a good man, she told us, kind and gentle, but she would cry herself to sleep at night and wear her wedding dress to play with the other neighbourhood girls, because she was still just a kid herself and didn't know any better, didn't know how to be a wife. Life as a young newlywed did not get any easier. She had two daughters in two years, Helen and Virginia, but Virginia died of spinal meningitis at the age of two, and her husband died not long after that.

Broke, alone and with few prospects in a state that offered her no future, Ma did what so many other widowed women of the day would do—she packed up Helen and moved home, to Montana, to be with her family. She got a job as a dishwasher at the Murray Hospital in Butte and worked long, hard hours to help provide for Helen.

Every day, she would tell us, she would walk to and from work past a fire station, where she would stop and chat with the firefighters, one day catching the eye of Robert Delich, a handsome young firefighter who had come to Butte from South Dakota. They courted for a time and then married, and the family soon followed: Robert Jr. arrived in 1938, and I was born on February 24, 1940. But theirs was a troubled union. Daddy was a drinker, and Ma had no emotional tools or economic choices to help her cope with him, or us. She was, I know now, scared to death of everything.

We lived in a four-room flat, kitty-corner to Grant Elementary, where I went to school. The rent was $27.50 a month, and Robert and I shared a bedroom. By then, Ma was working at the American Grill in town, washing dishes and cleaning chickens, her hands perpetually scarlet, chapped raw and scratched up from the scalding water and sharp chicken bones. Sometimes, she would bring cakes, vanilla and chocolate, home from the restaurant and let us eat them for breakfast, with coffee. But she was such an unhappy woman, always telling us that she was born under an unlucky star. For a time, we had to go on welfare, a necessary but humiliating experience for

The Delich family—my father Robert, my mother Josephine, my brother Robert Jr. and me at the age of three—taken in 1943 when my father was stationed in Arizona.

Ma. One Christmas, there were donated gifts under the tree, and even though I didn't much care that my doll had stains on her clothing and chips out of her face, and even though my brother didn't much care that the Tinkertoy set he opened was full of broken sticks and wooden parts with peeling paint, Ma cried when she saw them.

Daddy was an alcoholic even before they married, and in 1944, he went AWOL from the U.S. Army. When the officials finally caught up with him, he had tuberculosis. Once, Ma took Robert and me—I was only five—on a train to visit him in the veterans' hospital in Walla Walla, Washington. It had shiny linoleum floors and lots of woodwork, but Daddy looked so sick, and we weren't allowed to even kiss him. When he recovered and moved back home, he stopped drinking for a time, perhaps because my mother became pregnant with Jerri, who was born in 1950, when I was ten. Daddy got a job in construction for the city, tried his hand at local politics and even joined the Masonic Lodge. For a time, life in the Delich house took on a normalcy.

Daddy was always a sweet man and never lost his temper. He didn't have a mean bone in his body and used to affectionately call me "pidge," which was short for little pigeon. But he was the kind of father who never talked, who never really connected with his kids. Even though he was there, he wasn't really there for us.

One night, he didn't come home, and Ma just sat staring out the window. She said: "He's not home," and I thought, "Oh God." We knew right away. He had started drinking again. Years later, I would puzzle over that decision, because when Daddy was in the Masonic Lodge, he was a respected member and even rose to the thirty-third degree of the association. He wore a ring with a big G in the centre, and whenever we asked what it stood for, he would say "George." We found out later that it was for "God." And that the tenets of the Masonic Lodge include teaching eternal redemption by living a clean life. He had managed to stop drinking for five years, and we never knew why he started again, but I said my prayers every night, asking God to look after me, to make sure my life would be better.

It was a terrible time. Daddy would be gone all day, and then show up at dinnertime with these big salami sausages from the delicatessen and breads and cheeses, and after we all ate, he would go to bed and sleep it off, the smell of alcohol reeking throughout the room. My brother was always so quiet, because he was upset about everything going on around him.

Through it all, Ma never wavered on how her children would be raised. She was strict beyond reason, not physically but emotionally. That's just the way it was, and even though I resented it and puzzled over it, I was never really given a choice. Nor did I question it much, or ask why I couldn't use the phone to call my school friends, why I could only go to the movies on Saturdays with Robert, why I couldn't join Brownies or Girl Scouts or sports teams or attend extracurricular events at school.

Ma's relationship with my half-sister, Helen, was challenging, too. Helen was rebellious, right through her teens, and never gave Ma a moment's peace. As she grew older and married, Helen continued to have difficulties with all her relationships, and even lost visitation rights and contact with her young sons, Terry and Gary, after she drifted away from her husband, Frank, a wonderful man who was so good to her.

During all our family turmoil, I looked to school as a haven. It was my constant, my grounding. I loved it. I wanted to excel in everything, be good at everything. I would volunteer to clean blackboards and then go to the boiler room to clean the erasers. I'd run errands for the teachers and go out to the store for supplies and cans of soup for the teachers' lunches.

My teachers, who seemed to know the struggle I was having at home, would sometimes ask why I couldn't join my schoolmates on field trips and after-school events, but I could only tell them that my mother would always just say, "Because I said so." Once, I stayed behind after school when I shouldn't have, because I wanted to go to a Brownies meeting, and Ma marched right into the classroom and hauled me out by the arm and took me home. I cried and asked why, and the answer was more of the same: "Because I said so."

And, of course, the more Ma kept me from being involved, the more involved I tried to be. I was a spelling bee champ, won awards for penmanship and led the class in Christmas carols, because, for me, it was all about the music.

I have been singing ever since I could remember. When I was in Grade 1, before the end of the school day, the teacher would often say, "Beverly, would you like to get up and sing?" and I would get up and sing. I wanted to be in every school play and tried out for them all, always for the lead, in every grade. I learned to tap dance and twirl the baton, and I was never happier than when I could dress up in a costume. I liked sports, too: baseball and basketball and Ping-Pong, all of which I could play during school hours but not on the teams after school.

If there was a bright light in the family for us three kids, it was my Bubba Mary, who was my father's mother and lived right across the lane from us. Ma didn't have a good relationship with our grandmother, and we could never figure out why, because she was such a sweet, kind woman. We loved visiting her because she had a great laugh and there were always toys in the yard for us to play with, a scooter and a wagon, and she fed us treats, such as cookies and Twinkies and Ding Dongs.

Bubba Mary's youngest son, our uncle Chris, lived with her. He had never married and was an alcoholic, too, which was just something Bubba Mary seemed to accept. He was a lot like Daddy, mild-mannered and good to us, and we liked being around him, even though his breath always smelled like alcohol. He'd give us "horsey" rides on his knee and play tag with us all over the house.

My other grandmother, Bubba Annie, lived nearby, too, but like my two grandfathers, who died when I was very young, my memories of her are faint. She seemed an unhappy woman, who seldom smiled and was critical of everything. She always wore black dresses with an apron over top. I was twelve when she died, and I remember my mother racing down the back alley screaming and crying, carrying Jerri in her arms.

Sometimes, as a special treat, Ma would pack a lunch and we would take a bus to the Columbia Gardens, about three kilometres east of Butte. It was paradise to Robert,

Jerri and me, a lush green park that shone like a jewel on the edges of the grimy, polluted environment that was the legacy of Butte's smelter industries. The gardens covered many acres, and there were pavilions and a boardwalk with concession stands selling hot taffy, homemade pastries, popcorn and fried chicken. The amusement park had a roller coaster, merry-go-round and one of the country's biggest Ferris wheels, and around every corner were trees and shrubs shaped like deer and cacti and even Mickey Mouse. It all looked and smelled wonderful to us kids, and those expeditions to Columbia Gardens were among the rare times we were truly happy and carefree.

Bubba Mary loved my brother, Robert—he was her shining star—and she helped us out a lot in those years. She even gave my parents the money for a down payment on a little house that cost $2,000, and we could afford to buy a car, the family's first, a Ford coupe, though we didn't have it long before we lost it because we couldn't pay the bills.

And then Daddy got cancer, when I was seventeen. It was a lump in his neck, with smaller lumps under his dentures that soon spread to his lungs. Bubba Mary paid for him to go to the Mayo Clinic in Minnesota, but the doctors were not optimistic and told Daddy to get his affairs in order, because he wasn't expected to live more than six more months. He came home and grew sicker, slowly turning into a skeleton. His hair went pure white, and when I came home from school, he would be sitting in a chair in his pajamas, so sick and quiet and sad, but he always asked me how my day was.

One day, Daddy went into the bathroom and suffered a hemorrhage. There were blood clots everywhere. He lay down on the floor, and we called the ambulance. When they stood him up, walked him through the door and lifted him onto the stretcher, his face was grey and sunken, his eyes bulging from their sockets. My mother went with him to the hospital, and during the night, she came home and told us, plain and simple: "He's gone."

There was never much communication in our family. It was yes, no and because I said so, for everything. We never talked about our feelings and didn't really know what to do or say when bad things happened. The night Daddy died, Robert went quiet and crumpled up in the twin bed across from mine, a nineteen-year-old man sobbing into his pillow.

The funeral was hard. Our Serbian Orthodox religion dictated that the service should be a big affair and that the coffin would be open. We all had to sit there, looking at Daddy in that stiff wooden box and thinking how alive he looked, like he could just get up from this nap and walk away. He was only forty-seven.

It was especially hard for Bubba Mary. She had already buried one son—Uncle Chris had died a year earlier, also from cancer—and it was a heartbreaking time for her. Eight years after Daddy's funeral, she died of breast cancer.

We slowly adjusted to Daddy's death. We missed him, but not much changed in our lives. We still never seemed to have enough money for the basics, so I got a part-time job during my senior year of high school, working a few days a week at the phone company as a long-distance switchboard operator.

And music was still my everything.

In high school, I had joined the student choir and several other smaller singing groups. One was called the Harmonettes, another was the Melloteens, and I sang duets and solos. Our groups were often invited to sing in public, and Ma would occasionally relent and let me participate. Sometimes, we had out-of-town meets and my teachers would convince Ma to let me go, usually to the University of Montana in Missoula, about two hundred kilometres southwest of Butte. It was a beautiful campus, dense with trees and nestled in the foothills. The tall, traditional buildings were sheathed in ivy that changed colours with the seasons. During the breaks, we would take walks through the grounds, and I would envision the day I would go to school there, living at the dorm and participating in all of the activities of college life, the football games, the gymnasium mixers, the student council, the social life.

With my graduation ceremony at Butte High School around the corner, Ma and I went shopping for a new outfit to mark the occasion. We chose an off-white linen two-piece suit. The skirt fell just below the knee and had a slit up the back. The jacket had pearl buttons and a stand-up Nehru collar. We decided that a strand of pearls would be the better choice than a blouse. The shoes were a point of contention: I wanted high heels and was insistent, despite Ma's protests. She relented, and I chose pale pink pearl heels with open toes and ankle straps. I could barely walk in them across the carpet in the store, but they were beautiful, and I was so happy. The outfit was perfect, but walking on the gymnasium's concrete floor during the ceremony was difficult, and all three of us—Ma and Robert were watching in the stands—held our breath as I gingerly made my way to pick up my diploma. We didn't have post-ceremony plans, because Ma wouldn't let me go to any parties and wanted me to come right home, which was the last thing I wanted to do. It was decided I could join a friend at a nearby restaurant for dinner, but it was a somewhat deflating end to what should have been a highlight of my life.

After graduation, I started working full-time, and within a year was promoted to supervisor, and I continued to give all my earnings to Ma. So did Robert, who worked for Consolidated Freightways. It was always the family's goal that, being the man in the family, he would one day go to university.

I loved my job, and working with dozens of other young single women at the Mountain States Telephone Company opened up a new world for me. Suddenly, at eighteen, I had friends and was socializing, and I loved it. I became the organizer for the staff parties, for every wedding shower and birthday, and went dining and dancing with my friends. It was the late 1950s, and I had discovered high heels, bouffant hair and cherry Coke. I was close to my first cousin, Mona, whose mother was Aunt Stella, Ma's sister. Mona and I hung out a lot. We would go to church together and always looked forward to going to breakfast after.

And I sang. I sang every chance I could get, encouraged by my friends and learning every new song on the radio so that I was ready for the next party and dance, for the next microphone around the next corner. I was singing all the time.

One of our favourite places to hang out was Luigi's, and a bunch of us girls would go there every week after work. The place was small, just a bar really. There was no food but lots of tables and booths. And booze. Luigi would sit at the front of the room, a one-man band. He sang and played the drum and cymbals and harmonica, and nearly every song was a polka. All the travelling salesmen who stopped over in Butte gravitated there, and we girls would dance the night away with them, with Luigi pounding out polkas. The place was unique...business cards and well wishes displayed everywhere, dancing spiders that would drop from the ceiling at any moment, animated moving objects and coloured lights flashing over the walls and ceiling. Sometimes, when one of us got up to go to the washroom, Luigi would stop playing and wait until we returned to our table before he started playing again. It was so embarrassing but such fun. Every once in a while, Luigi would take a break and join the bartender to serve drinks, but I always stuck to cherry Coke.

I took a shine to one of the salesmen, a Ukrainian from Ohio named Gerry, and he to me. He was a regular, and we loved dancing together. He would call me in advance and tell me he would be in town the following weekend. I'd iron my crinolines to get ready, and we'd spend Friday, Saturday and Sunday nights at Luigi's, dancing. Another favourite hangout was the Brown Jug on the southlands, where we would congregate in groups and dance the night away.

But I wanted more. More freedom. More control over my own life. I was still living at home, and although my mother's hold on me was beginning to loosen, I desperately wanted to be out on my own. It took a few years to work up my nerve, to find the right moment, but when I found that little apartment, in a nice renovated building, I never told anybody. I quietly put a deposit on it and then, one day, told Ma that I had to leave.

She was furious. She swore and called me names. Jerri, upset and confused, followed me around the house, crying. I loaded all my clothes and my shoe boxes in my little car, a Chevy Corvair, turned to my little sister as I was going out the front door, and said: "Don't cry, Jerri. I'll come and see you all the time." I'm sure Robert must have felt I was abandoning him, too.

Sister Jerri and me, right, taken in 1964.

I had done it, and I felt free. But even as my new life was unfolding, I kept my promise and went to see Ma and Jerri all the time. By then, Ma had become very sick with diabetes, and despite our strained relationship, I would go over to her house every morning, on my way to work, and give her a shot of insulin and it seemed to keep some kind of family peace. Ma would always ask me to come back home, but in her heart I believe she knew that I couldn't.

My apartment was one big room with a Murphy bed and a little kitchen, and the living space was just large enough that I could fit an organ in it, because that's what I'd always wanted to do: play the piano, or the organ. So I bought an organ and practised whenever I could. One day, there was a knock at the door, and when I opened it, the young man standing there said: "I wanted to see who was playing the organ above me, because I play the piano."

His name was Chuck Wright.

Chuck and I became the best of friends. He was five years younger than I, only nineteen, and he was a homosexual, but we had so much in common. We loved getting dressed up—me in my three-piece Italian knit suits, high heels and matching gloves, him in nice suits and ties.

We eventually fell in love, which might seem odd, but Chuck always said that he thought it didn't matter that he was gay. When we made the decision to get married, in 1964, it didn't sit well with Ma, or with my family or friends, but we were determined. We had a lovely wedding in a Catholic church. I wore a white dress, and my whole family was there, along with all my friends from the telephone company.

Chuck worked in a bank in Butte but before long began talking about moving to Missoula, because he wanted to take classes at the university. So we moved. He was such a smart man, almost professor-like, and taught me about worldly subjects, such as ancient history and classical music. Once we were in Missoula, it didn't take long for me to find a job: my work experience helped me land a supervising position at the phone company, and we lived in a nice apartment on campus.

Ma's health continued to worsen, and in 1965, she passed away from kidney failure. She was only sixty. During her last year, it was difficult for Robert and Jerri. Robert was working and attending Montana Tech, so Jerri was the main caretaker at a young age. Helen, who still lived in Butte, wanted to take Jerri, who was then fifteen, but Robert said he wouldn't have it, because our relationship throughout our childhood with Helen was far from amicable (she passed away several years after Ma). Jerri wanted to finish school in Butte and opted to live with Aunt Stella for a short while, but it didn't work. She went to live with friends, which was also unsuitable, so we decided collectively that she needn't finish school in Butte and should come to live with Chuck and me. I was so happy to have her, because she had always been so dear to me. Chuck was okay with it, so we found a new apartment with two bedrooms, and Jerri moved to Missoula. My brother had sold our little family house in Butte and then moved to Missoula, too, so that he could go to university, which he had always wanted to do. Jerri settled into school, and our family was back together in a serendipitous if odd kind of way.

One day, three years after we got married, Chuck sat me down and we had a discussion about him fighting turmoil within. He was realizing that he wanted to live openly as a gay man. I wasn't surprised—we had been growing distant, and I think we both knew that it would someday happen—so we divorced but vowed to remain friends.

During the marriage, Jerri and I had become friendly with one of our neighbours. Al Holender was from Edmonton but had moved to Missoula to go to university, and he lived next door to us in the apartment building on Madison Avenue.

Al was a bit of a nut, but in a good way. He was Jewish, suffered from ulcers and had congenital cataracts, with clear vision in only one eye, and he always seemed to be sick. But he was a lot of fun. He used to ask me to fix him up with my single friends at the phone company, and they would complain to me afterward that he had tried to convert them to Judaism.

By the time Chuck and I split, Al had finished university and moved to Vancouver. I realized that I missed him, and it turned out that he missed me, too. When he asked me to fly out to the West Coast to see him, I did. It was Christmastime, and there was snow on the ground and a beautiful view from atop the Blue Horizon restaurant, where he took me to dinner. I fell in love with the city.

When I returned to Missoula after that fun weekend, I could scarcely keep my mind on my work. Several weeks later, Al called and said that he wasn't enjoying the dating scene and had been thinking that I should move to Vancouver and that we should get married.

"You and I were always good friends," he said, "and I don't see why it wouldn't work."

I paused, but only for a moment, and said yes.

It was 1967, and I was worried about leaving Jerri behind when I moved to Vancouver. She was nearly eighteen and was happy that I was going to marry Al, but she decided to stay in Missoula with a friend so that she could finish high school. Robert moved to Fort Benton with his wife, Ruth, whom he had married after both of them graduated from the University of Montana with teaching degrees. Jerri later moved to Fort Benton also, when a job offer became available at the grade school library.

When Al called his parents in Edmonton and told them he was going to marry me, they weren't exactly thrilled. His dad, Phil, told him he wanted to come to Vancouver to talk with him, or more precisely, talk him out of it. They had visited Al in Missoula, so they knew that I was married to Chuck and that I wasn't Jewish, which meant I had two strikes against me: I was divorced and a shiksa. But Al told them we were getting married, with or without their approval, and asked them to come to the wedding. They did.

Al's mom, Clare, had recently lost her father and cried through the whole ceremony. I wasn't sure if she was crying because she lost her father or because Al was marrying me, but it was probably a combination of both. We exchanged our vows on December 3, 1967, in front of a rabbi in our apartment, with Al's childhood buddy Harry as his best man. Jerri came from Montana, to act as my witness and maid of honour, and I was so happy she was there. I had always felt bad about leaving her behind in Butte, as if I was abandoning her for the second time, but she said it never bothered her and that she was happy that I was living my life the way I wanted to.

It had taken Al three tries to find a rabbi who would conduct the service. The Orthodox and Conservative rabbis that he had approached declined, but he finally found a Reform rabbi who agreed—but only if I promised to convert to Judaism and join his synagogue.

I agreed.

I had read up on Judaism and realized there was nothing I couldn't handle about the religion, and I wasn't that committed to my Serbian Orthodox upbringing anyway, having not really been involved with it since my teen years. So I started going to conversion classes, and I loved it. I adored the rabbi and met wonderful people, who helped with the transition. Most of all, I relished the camaraderie, the feeling of family and caring and the Jewish "sisterhood" and the way I was welcomed by what seemed like the entire Vancouver Jewish community.

Judaism suddenly became a new way of life for me, though I've since come to realize that it's never really been about the religion itself. I have always prayed to God, but Judaism was, for me, about a newfound sense of belonging.

And, of course, I joined the choir, becoming the soloist at Temple Sholom. The congregation began calling me the "Singing Angel," and before long, the rabbi asked me to perform as a cantorial soloist, which was a great honour. Our choir had a very special bond. There were approximately a dozen of us. We would go out after rehearsals and have such a good time that sometimes the place would be closing up and the staff would be cleaning the floors around our feet. We decided to bring our own goodies, and soon the spread afterward was more like a banquet, with baked salmon, salads, buns and desserts. We also went on overnight trips to various communities and cities to perform.

And life with Al was never dull. We laughed a lot and had many friends and an active social life. His eyesight was always an issue and he wasn't permitted to drive, so I did all the driving, but nothing slowed us down.

The first couple we met in Vancouver, through Al's volunteer work at the YMCA, was Marit and Jon Henderson. Marit had come from Norway to work for a year as a nurse. She met Jon, who was a teacher, and when she went back to Norway, he later followed her and asked her dad for permission to marry her. They came back to Vancouver to live, which was hard for her, being so far from her family, but they were so in love with each other. They married, had two boys and our families became inseparable. From the moment I met Marit, we just clicked: instant best friends. Always level-headed and straightforward, she was the one who helped keep my "noisy" life, as she called it, on track.

Al's vision continued to be a challenge for him, but he was a trooper and never let it slow him down. He did his master's work in sociology at the University of British Columbia and worked for the Vancouver park board before landing a job as executive director for Big Brothers at the Burnaby branch. Putting his degree to good use, he also did marriage counselling on the side.

I was working as a switchboard operator at Mainland Foundry, and Al's parents gave us the money for a down payment, so we bought a little house in Burnaby, for $17,000. When I got pregnant with our daughter, Lisa, I quit my job and concentrated on our growing family. When Lisa was born, in 1969, we moved to a slightly bigger home in south Vancouver.

In 1971, our son, Daniel, was born. I wanted to renovate to make room for our new son, because I loved the South Cambie area, but Al wanted something new in the suburbs, so we moved again, this time to Richmond. We had many friends and a great social life with lots of house parties. The music would come on, ABBA would start the night, and everyone would jump onto the dance floor. One of our favourite evenings out was at the dinner club Paesano's in a little strip mall on No. 3 Road. Mamma cooked in the kitchen and her sons, Joseph and Tony, ran the business, hosting, serving and making sure everyone was having a great time. We would always go into the kitchen and hug Mamma, which seemed to make her night. Most weekends there was a musical duo, an accordion player and a guitarist, who came around to the tables and serenaded the patrons. Whenever they came to our table, my friends would persuade me to sing with them, and I would usually croon one of my favourite tunes, "Vaya con Dios."

Our house was in a new subdivision and was just one of the hundreds of big houses filling up with young families. The kids went to Grauer Elementary School and thrived. Daniel took up hockey and baseball, and Lisa took to figure skating, cheerleading and baseball, too. Al's dad, Phil, finished the rec room in our basement, and I was handy with a jigsaw. When we were done, our new party room had tongue-and-groove oak panelling, a stone fireplace and a leather-trimmed wet bar.

In 1976, Jerri married the "love of her life," Bill Gertson, in a beautiful ceremony in Coeur d'Alene, Idaho. It took her twenty-six years to find him, and he was the blessing that now came to give her all the happiness that she deserved. We were all so happy for her.

In the fall of 1978, I drove down with Al to attend my twenty-year high school reunion. When we checked into our hotel, I realized I had left behind my two party dresses in a garment bag on the back of the closet door. One was for the Friday night reception and one for the Saturday bash, so I had to go shopping and pick up something to wear. I went to an upscale boutique in town called Thomas's and luckily found not one, but two dresses. The first was a long yellow crepe dress with thin straps and a lacy appliqué on the bodice, and the other was a three-quarter-length satin number with spaghetti straps and alternating black and white layers. They were

A photograph of me performing at my twenty-year high school reunion in 1978. My love of music began with singing, but eventually expanded into coaching and artist management.

perfect, mostly because they showed off the tan I had been working on so diligently in the months before the reunion.

The weekend was a blast, and no one was more surprised than I when I was awarded Most Changed Woman, an accolade no doubt prompted by the fact that I was thinner, had a tan, didn't wear glasses anymore and had a trendy curly Afro-style hairdo, à la Barbra Streisand in *A Star Is Born*. As I was getting ready to leave, just before midnight on the Saturday, I ran into one of the "cute" boys from high school. He asked why I was leaving so soon, and I laughed and said: "I'm going home, like Cinderella, before I turn into a pumpkin... and where were you when I needed you in high school?"

On a sadder note, it was difficult to visit the area where I had grown up and gone to elementary school. The Anaconda Copper Mining Company had turned the entire site into open-pit mining, and our beloved Columbia Gardens had succumbed to the same destiny.

Al was always a supportive husband. One day he handed me a magazine about home decor and said: "Listen, this is something you'd be really great at, because you're so good at decorating and fixing up the house."

It was a story about Decorating Den, a franchised company that specialized in mobile interior decor and design. Essentially, it was a door-to-door business that took the hassle out of home decorating by consulting, designing, delivering and installing everything, from drapes and carpets to furniture and accessories, for harried housewives who were filling up the suburbs across Canada and who had the money but not the time to feather their new nests.

It was right up my creative alley, the kind of job that was the perfect blend of independence, socializing and organization. Before I knew it, I had taken the company course in Indianapolis and owned the Decorating Den franchise for western Canada.

I was thirty-seven, I had a great family and, now, a promising business, so I set about knocking on doors in my Richmond neighbourhood. I learned the trade quickly, with the help of a good friend already in the decorating business, who was working as a textile supplier. I seemed to have a gift for interpreting the vision of clients, and soon the phone was ringing off the hook with client after client, who had heard about my work from a friend who loved what I had done to their living room/bedroom/rec room. I worked out of an office in my basement, hired an assistant who had been a previous client and business got better and better, until I had ten Decorating Den vans on the road, and my franchise was number one in sales in the country.

And then things began to fall apart.

It was 1980. My fortieth birthday was coming up, and I had made plans for a bash at our house, when, on the morning of the big day, Al woke up with no vision in his good eye. It was something doctors had warned him might come with time, something that he dreaded, for it meant a dangerous operation that he had been putting off for years, an operation that instead of restoring his sight could leave him totally blind. He had the procedure four days after my birthday, and it was a success: he ended up with 20/20 vision in the eye, and for the first time he could remember, he could see everything clearly. It was exciting, as if he had been reborn. He started going shopping for groceries just so that he could read the labels, and everyone who knew about his eye problems was so happy for him.

Al decided that he wanted to come into the Decorating Den business with me and left his job with Big Brothers.

It was an awkward time—I was the boss, and it was difficult to figure out how Al fit into the mix, being neither partner nor employee. He didn't have any experience in the business either, and we struggled to figure out our evolving personal and professional roles. The decorators were also less than infatuated with Al's involvement, and after a time, we mutually agreed that it was not working and he would have to find something else.

He got a plum job as a fundraiser at UBC, and for a while, things were going well. Lisa was preparing for her upcoming bat mitzvah, and Daniel was busy with his sports.

And then came the economic crash.

Al and I had remortgaged the house to start and build the business, and our accountant looked at the numbers and told us to prepare for the worst, but we didn't know how bad it would be until the business began to fall off. We lost our house and moved into a nearby rental home, and even though I tried everything to keep the business going, one day the phones just stopped ringing. It was 1981, two and a half years after I bought the franchise, and I had to walk away, had to let go of my decorators and other employees. It was devastating.

It wasn't long before I got another job, at an interior design company. It wasn't my own business, but it used my skills and helped pay the bills, and our financial tide began to turn.

And then came another bombshell.

One day, while we were sitting in the backyard, Al turned to me and said: "There's something I have to tell you. I have been having an affair." It wasn't his first confessed indiscretion, but for me it would be the last. I was furious and disappointed, and sad for the children, but I knew that this was it. I went out and bought a book titled How to Leave and prepared to do just that.

But I didn't leave then.

In the midst of our marital meltdown, Al was offered a job at the University of Alberta and asked me to move with him and the kids to Edmonton. At first, I adamantly refused, but I had been seeing a counsellor to help me deal with our faltering marriage, and he said: "Why don't you go and get away from everything here for a while? You can always come back."

I knew that I had reached a limit. I no longer loved or respected Al, and the kids were getting old enough to understand, if not accept, the divorce of their parents. I agreed.

We made plans to move, and shortly before heading east, I went out for a few drinks with a girlfriend. We were at a bar, talking about the move and my disintegrating marriage, when a man walked up to us and introduced himself. He was from Toronto and was with his son, and he wondered if I might like to dance. I did. All night long.

His name was Art, and he was fourteen years older than I, a handsome widower, and he danced like Fred Astaire. When he said, at night's end, "Can I walk you to your car?" I said yes, and when he said, "Can I kiss you?" I said yes.

It was electric.

A few days later, I said to my friend: "I am going to have an affair." And I did.

Art was upset when I told him I was moving to Edmonton, and he wanted to move there as well, so that we could be together. But I didn't think it was a good idea, so he stayed in Vancouver.

In 1983, we packed up the family and moved to Edmonton. We rented a beautiful home on Wahstao Crescent near the West Edmonton Mall. One day while hanging out at the mall, I wandered into a brand new decorating store called the Drapery Shop, part of a chain that originated in eastern Canada. I began talking to the staff and told them that I had just moved here from Vancouver. A manager came out and spoke with me as well. She told me that she was there temporarily and was looking for a store manager, because she needed to get back to head office. I told her I wasn't interested, but I would give it some thought. And I did think about it. I found the days long with the kids in school, so I took the position. It was a challenging job. The corporate manager stayed on for a brief time to train me, but there was much to learn and the days were long. It worked out well in that the kids would come after school and ice skate or partic- ipate in one of the many activities that the mall offered. The staff were more than supportive, and we were a good team. They were empathetic to the pressures I was under and would bring me chocolates from Purdy's, flowers and other special treats. Sadly, a year later, receivers showed up at the door and closed the store, much to everyone's shock.

Soon after that, I landed a sales position at Neon Products, designing and selling illuminated signage. The sales manager felt it would be a good fit with my design background. It was interesting and challenging, and I was assigned a great client list, including Kentucky Fried Chicken, Budweiser and several others.

Al and I were living in an uneasy state of detente, together but apart, friendly but not loving. It came time to plan Daniel's bar mitzvah, which was a welcome distraction. Family and friends from both Al's side and mine came, and it truly was a wonderful time. Al's dad had told his visiting relatives about our estrangement, and they tried to commiserate, but I wasn't up for any discussions. My mind was made up; when the time was right, I would leave.

I had been having anxiety attacks, which started before I went to Edmonton, and one episode in Vancouver had been so bad that I went to the hospital. I felt as if I was totally disconnected from myself, and even though I had been getting counselling, it was all piling up: the move to Edmonton, my failing marriage and Al's health—he'd been diagnosed with Crohn's disease after our marriage and had several attacks over the past few years. I couldn't believe my life was in such disarray. The anxiety seemed to go away once we settled in Edmonton, once I started working, but I knew it was nature's way of telling me that, even if I looked fine on the outside, inside I was a mess.

I had told Al about my affair with Art, because there was nothing between us anymore except the marriage and the children. I think I knew then that even though we could have had a comfortable family life in Edmonton, I was done. I continued to see Art. He would come to Edmonton to see me, or we would meet halfway in Calgary. It was a strange, surreal way to live—me having an open affair while Al and I were still living together—and I grew unhappier. Al knew it and, after a year and a half, he told me that he wasn't going to stay at the university and we should move back to Vancouver. We had taken the kids out for dinner, and afterward Al took them home, but I went to a local piano bar in Edmonton and sang the night away. I hadn't been that happy in a long time.

Lisa was away at summer camp when Al drove back to Vancouver with Daniel. Art flew to Edmonton to drive me back, and in the car, I began talking about what things had been like for me in those last few days of my life in Alberta. He turned to me and said: "I don't want to talk about your marriage anymore. I want to talk about us." That threw me. Suddenly it wasn't about an affair; it was about something more concrete. It was as though I abruptly had to make a choice. My head was spinning. I wasn't even separated. What was I going to do? And how was I going to do it?

In Vancouver, Al and I moved into a duplex behind the Oakridge shopping centre. I lived upstairs with Lisa and Daniel, and Al lived in the downstairs suite. We would remain friends, but both of us knew that the marriage was over.

I found the readjustment to life in Vancouver harder than I had expected. I was still unsettled, and it was diffi-cult to be around our married friends, the ones we had always socialized with as a couple. I couldn't return to Temple Sholom because it, too, felt strange, and I didn't want to talk about my separation from Al or my new and different life. And I was struggling with my relationship with Art.

One evening, Art and I were out dancing when he looked at me, with sadness in his eyes, and said: "I don't think you realize it, but you're pulling away from me." I denied it, but a few days later, he said it again: "Darling, you don't realize it. But you're pulling away."

And I was. I had been ever since that car ride home.

One night, at his place, I admitted to him what had once been unthinkable to me: "You're right, I can't do it. And I can't even explain why." He never said a word. Not one word. I left, and for a brief time, I felt a weight had been lifted off my shoulders, but several weeks later, I broke down, not believing what I had done, not understanding why I had pushed away this man who had meant so much to me.

I called him and asked if he would meet with me one more time, for a drink, and when he sat down, he said: "You know that it's taken everything that I own to be able to sit across from you." I told him I was sorry that I hurt him, that I needed to get my life in order, that nothing made sense to me at present. Neither of us wanted to prolong the agony, and so we parted for good. I would see him again, once, nine years later at the Pacific National Exhibition, where I was working. I looked up and saw him watching me from across the room. I went over and hugged him, and he said: "Look at you, still in charge of everything."

In 1986, Al and I agreed that our finances were more stable, so we could make the separation official. I helped him move into an apartment down the street so that he could stay close to our children. He wanted Daniel to come and live with him, but I felt it was too soon, that one separation was enough for the children at that time. I proceeded to legally revert to my maiden name, Delich.

I didn't know it then, but not fifteen kilometres away, an eleven-year-old Burnaby boy named Michael Bublé, who loved hockey and slept every night with his Bible and grew up listening to his grandfather's jazz records, was starting to find his voice.

My new life was about to begin.

CHAPTER TWO

Fifteen Per Cent of Nothing

After Al moved out into his own apartment, I got a job at Neon Products, the company I had worked for in Edmonton. Owned by B.C. billionaire Jimmy Pattison, it wasn't exactly a progressive place, at least not in the 1980s and not when it came to hiring women, who seldom held senior positions.

But my previous experience seemed to make a difference, so they gave me a job as the only female salesperson on their force, making it clear that it was because they wanted to use the training they had already invested in me. It was a tough slog. I had to go out and pound the pavement, selling signage without a client list, which I'd had in Edmonton and which all the male salespeople in Vancouver had. It was difficult to get a foothold and land clients, and I realized the job just wasn't a good fit for me, but times were unsettled, as they always are after a marriage breakdown, and I had to adjust to my new reality. I needed to work and make my own way.

Although Al was still part of our lives, I was learning how to adapt to being a single working mom, something that was becoming less unusual after our divorce in 1986, as the post-feminist generation spawned a new social demographic marked by high divorce rates and more and more one-parent households.

One night, a friend and I went for dinner at Mingles, a restaurant on Broadway. Earlier in the week, I had driven by and noticed that the restaurant needed signage, which meant I might be able to make a sale, so I had gone in and the hostess told me the manager wouldn't be in for a few days. "Do you remember the Platters?" she said. "Well, one of them is the manager." She suggested I come back and talk to him, so my friend and I decided to have dinner and maybe drum up some business for me at the same time.

The manager's name was Ray Carroll, and it turned out that not only did he run the restaurant; he also entertained the customers, and on the day we went, he was singing. Afterward, the hostess pointed him in our direction, and he came over and introduced himself. We began discussing the possibility of a sign for the restaurant. And then my friend said to him: "Do you know that Beverly sings?" I told him I was out of practice and excused myself to go the ladies room. While I was gone, I later found out, Ray had asked my friend if I was married. "Yes, she's happily married," she said, not wanting to tell him that I was just separated and was coming off an affair. She wanted to protect me.

When I came back to the table, Ray asked me to sing, and after a bit of prompting from them both, I did. I don't remember what exactly, but it was either "Edelweiss" or "Cabaret," two of my favourite songs and the ones I usually sang impromptu.

Ray asked me to come by the restaurant later in the week so that we could talk about a sign, and when I showed up a few days later with a miniature light box version of the sign I thought would be perfect, he showed little interest and instead asked me out to dinner. It annoyed me, and I told him so: "I'm not into that. Look I've just been separated, and I just ended an affair, and my head is not on straight. I'm just here for the business, so if you're not interested…" And I got up.

"No, no, no," he said, "I would be interested, and I'm sorry."

I left, and followed up with him later, but he never did buy the sign.

After a few months, I left Neon Products and found myself back in the decorating business, working in North Vancouver as the manager of Contour Canada, a store that sold window products and fabrics. I changed the staff around and started to run things my way. I had six salespeople and two installers working for me, and soon our store was one of the highest-earning franchises in the Canada-wide chain.

And then one day, a phone call came into the office for me. It was Ray Carroll. He had contacted Neon Products, and they had directed him to my new workplace.

"Beverly, this is Ray. Is your head on straight yet?"

I laughed and said, "Yes, as a matter of fact, it is." He asked me to dinner, and I said yes.

Ray was fourteen years older than I—single, charming, interesting and very funny. He was with the Platters and toured and recorded with the group during the 1950s, taking the place of one of the members who had left the original band. He was an American citizen from Chicago but owed a huge U.S. tax bill, so he decided to move north to Canada, performing in Toronto and Montreal, working and singing at restaurants, before making his way to Vancouver. He had an adult daughter, Kim, who lived in Montreal, and she and I hit it off from the moment we met.

Ray and I soon became an item, but I thought he was wasting his talent singing at various restaurants around town and began urging him to put together a new Platters tribute group. He was considering it, when a good friend and talent agent Lyvia Smith called and said that a promoter she knew was looking to put a tour together of a few groups from the 1950s. One of the groups would be the Platters, and was he interested? He was, so we began holding auditions. We found a terrific female singer and another local fellow, but there weren't a lot of black men in Vancouver at that time, and the group needed four people. With Ray, we had only three.

We were still looking for the fourth singer but decided to take the two new members to Seattle for a photo shoot so that we could at least start promoting what we had. Just before we were to start the session, I turned to Ray and said: "Why don't I just go out on the street and find a good-looking black man that we can use in the picture temporarily?"

He thought it was a great idea, so there I was, standing on the corner checking out all the men walking down the street and in the crosswalks. And then, there he was, walking toward me, a tall, gorgeous black man in a trench coat. I approached him, quickly explained our situation, and he was so amused by the story that he agreed to pose for us. In return, I sent him a picture as a souvenir.

The newly reconstituted Platters—Ray, Gloria, Sonny and Umeme, whom we'd finally added to make up the quartet—went on a twenty-seven-day B.C. Legends of Rock and Roll tour in 1987, with some other oldie-but-goodie retro acts, including the Coasters, Bobby Curtola and Buddy Knox. The tour was a huge hit, with the final performance at Club 86 at the old Expo site. Afterward,

This picture of the Platters tribute band was taken for the Legends of Rock and Roll tour in 1987. From left: Gloria, Ray, Sonny, me and Umeme. Ray and I were business partners at the time.

Ray convinced me to leave Contour and come work with him in the entertainment industry.

He thought we'd be good business partners, saying, "I can tell you're a good business woman, there's no BS with you. You're straight down the line, and I will teach you the business."

So I left my job at Contour, and Ray and I formed Del-Carr Entertainment, a talent agency. We found a place on Cook Street near Second Avenue in False Creek, a second-storey office space with a huge warehouse out back. We decorated it and held an open house and invited all our friends but no one from the local entertainment industry, because at that point we didn't really have many contacts. My friend, the one who had been with me the night I met Ray, was at the party, and she came up to me, looked around the place and said in amusement: "Well, this is very interesting, Bev, and I'd throw some business your way if I knew what the hell the business was."

Ray began scouting, and we eventually signed a few acts and booked them. We'd get 15 per cent of whatever the acts made. And that's how we started.

The Platters continued to perform, and our business began to flourish. We had more clients and invested ourselves full bore into Del-Carr. Ray directed and I even produced a musical revue titled *Blast from the Past*, which was based on a 1950s musical playing in Las Vegas, though our show at the Waterfront Theatre featured local singers and dancers.

Del-Carr was beginning to make a name for itself in the local entertainment industry.

On the morning of December 19, 1989, I was sitting

at home when I got a call from our good friend Sibel Thrasher, who had just driven by our office. She said: "Bev, your building is on fire." I called Ray and we drove over to the building, and there it was: the entire building destroyed. All of our stuff, our instruments, sound equipment, files, photos, records and decorations—all of it—up in flames. We had nothing left. And we had no insurance. I don't know why, because it wasn't like me to not have insurance, but somehow we never got around to it.

After the ashes settled, our friend Sylvia Russell, who ran the Vancouver food bank, offered to let us restart the business in some offices she wasn't using, but I told Ray I was done. It was as if the wind had gone out of my sails, so I went to work at a telemarketing company downtown, where I supervised the sale of lottery tickets. Ray was devastated, because he didn't know what to do either, so he continued performing with the Platters while we tried to figure out what came next.

It turned out to be the business of talent contests, maybe not the *American Idol* kind but talent contests nonetheless, mostly held in clubs around town that welcomed them as a way to get people in the door and sell more drinks. The truth is, everyone loves a talent contest, and even though the prizes were small, we managed to book a lot of them, and they drew big crowds.

About the same time, a friend told me about a job at the Pacific National Exhibition, the venerable annual fair held every August on the Hastings Park site in East Vancouver. It was a part-time contract to coordinate community entertainment, specifically a youth talent search program, which sounded perfect for me. I took in a resume and was hired on the spot. The pay was $7,000 for the seventeen-day fair, and I was to start working that spring in preparation for the 1990 fair.

Things were looking up. Lisa was in school in Toronto for merchandising management, and Daniel, just out of high school and following his dream to become a pilot, was busy preparing submissions for aviation schools.

And I had a new job, a job that seemed tailor-made for me.

I was in the shower one morning in early January when I noticed bleeding from the nipple on my left breast. I had always been in terrific health but knew enough to have it checked out. The doctor couldn't find anything unusual but sent me for a mammogram. It showed a small spot. I had a biopsy on a Friday morning and the following Monday was on the phone scheduling an appointment with a surgeon.

It was breast cancer. I was just about to turn fifty.

To celebrate my birthday, Ray and I had planned a cruise to the Caribbean in late February with twenty or so friends, and I wasn't going to miss it. So with my doctors' permission, we went on the seven-day sail, knowing that when we returned I would be going right into surgery.

I knew it was going to be a tough road ahead, but with most adversities in my life, my spirituality has been a guide, and this time was no exception.

On the recommendation of a good friend, Ray and I had recently become devotees of Reverend Ernie Forks, who was the minister of a new Vancouver church called Science of Mind, which taught spiritual mind treatment, or affirmative prayer. It had a New Age feel to it, but its philosophies, such as "talk as if and act as if," made sense to me, especially the emphasis on the power of positive thinking.

Once, when Ray and I were having dinner with the reverend, I confided in him that I'd had the biopsy.

"How did that go?" he said.

"I have cancer."

He looked at me and said, "Do you want to be well?"

I said: "Of course."

"Then you are well," he said.

We went to services every Sunday at the Masonic Lodge in Marpole, and we would sing, me leading the congregation in hymns and songs like "Hello," which came from a movie called *Crazy People* about a man in a psychiatric hospital who collects cut-outs of the word "hello" in a box and then hands them out to patients. I did the same thing, and my Hello Box soon became a Sunday tradition at the Science of Mind church.

I had the cancer surgery, a lumpectomy, in March and afterward went for radiation three times a week for about five weeks, at the Vancouver General Hospital cancer clinic. I didn't mind the treatments, which were painless, but resented being away from my new job, even though my bosses at the PNE were great about it. In fact, they told me I couldn't come to work until I had clearance from my doctors. That's when it really sunk in that I had cancer. I cried until I could scarcely breathe and then pulled myself together, vowing to make the most of my recovery. I read books and magazines, did crosswords, caught up with family and friends and, after three weeks, went back to work.

But it was tiring, because I was still getting radiation treatments, and sometimes, I would call Ray early in the day and ask him to come and get me. He was wonderful. He would pick me up and take me home, and after the fair that year, I gave him a framed certificate that said: "In Appreciation For Driving Miss Daisy."

I loved working at the PNE, and even though I started out with the responsibility for the Youth Talent Search, the Kids' Talent Search and the ever-so-fun Extra Years of Zest Talent Search, my role gradually expanded as the years went on.

During the months between fairs, Ray and I continued with our talent contests around town, and in 1993, we found ourselves holding court one night at the Big Bamboo nightclub on Broadway.

We'd convinced the club owner to let us do the contest, that it was a great way to bring in people and, in turn, sell liquor. We'd get a percentage from the door. I was the organizer, and Ray was one of the judges. One of the other judges I had asked to join us for the week-night contest, held in the club's upstairs tiki-style room, was Hugh Pickett, by then a well-known local impresario, who had made a name for himself by bringing big acts like Mitzi Gaynor and Bette Midler to Vancouver venues such as the Cave Supper Club.

I got to know Hugh when Ray and I were booking the Platters around town, because Hugh would come to all the shows. He was enigmatic and charming, though very private, aloof in a way, and always said whatever was on his mind, because he really didn't care what others thought about him. We hit it off instantly and became life-long friends.

One of the contestants that night at the Big Bamboo was a good-looking young man wearing a white T-shirt and blue jeans. He had signed up to sing "It Had to Be You," a 1924 standard, but as we were busy preparing to start the evening, he was becoming more and more impatient and kept coming over to the judges' table, leaning over Hugh and me and bugging us about when the show would start. It was starting to annoy Hugh, who kept turning to me and said, through the pursed lips he was so well known for, "Who is that?"

"It's Michael Bublé," I told him. "He's one of the contestants."

There were about ten performers that night, and they used recorded music—the contestants had to come with background tapes—and when Michael got up onstage and sang, everybody in the club went crazy. He took the microphone off the stand and was moving all over the stage and had such a beautiful, smooth voice and a strong presence, his voice somewhere between Elvis Presley and Frank Sinatra. He was slim, with high pompadour-style hair, and so full of energy.

Hugh turned to me, lips pursed again, and said: "Who is this?"

And I said, "Oh my God." We didn't know what to think. Except that, clearly, Michael Bublé was the winner.

Turned out there was a little problem, though, which I hadn't caught during the registration process and didn't notice until after everyone had performed, after we had picked Michael as the winner.

Michael couldn't win, because he wasn't old enough. I discussed it with Hugh, and we agreed we had to stick to the rules, so I had to go over and tell our winner that he wasn't the winner. Michael was sitting with some friends in a booth on the other side of the club, laughing and talking.

"Michael," I said, "I've got some good news and some bad news. How old are you?"

"Eighteen."

"Okay, the good news is that you've won the contest, but the bad news is that you're not even supposed to be in here. You're not nineteen, and this is a club, so I have to disqualify you. I'm on the line here, and this is illegal."

He was really upset. The prize was an unusually big one, a trip to *The Arsenio Hall Show* and $1,000 in cash. But I couldn't make an exception and told him so. He went home empty-handed and, as I would find out much later, told his parents, Amber and Lewis, the whole story, including the part about "Beverly the bitch," who disqualified him.

It would be a while before our paths would cross again.

My contract at the PNE continued to be renewed—I ended up working there for eleven seasons—and I eventually took over responsibilities for all the community entertainment at the fair. I loved the job and I was good at it, and every year the crowds coming to the talent shows at the fairground grew and grew.

Michael, meanwhile, was working with his dad, Lewis, on the family fishing boat and at a Richmond rock climbing club that the family owned.

He had always sung, starting when he was small, even

dreaming at the age of two that he would become famous. Michael was the oldest of the three Bublé siblings, with sisters Brandee and Crystal rounding out the close-knit Italian family. He learned to love jazz at an early age, influenced by the singing greats his parents played on the family stereo and by his grandfather Mitch's collection of jazz records. And although he also liked rock and roll, it was listening to a group like the Mills Brothers, he said, that took him to another place. At thirteen, during a family singalong to Bing Crosby's "White Christmas," it was clear that young Michael had a gift. He began performing in and around Vancouver at the urging of Mitch, who was a plumber and not only paid for his singing lessons but also offered free plumbing services to club owners and musicians in exchange for letting his grandson perform.

Michael loved hockey as much as he loved music, once saying that if he couldn't be a professional ice hockey player—playing on a team like his beloved Vancouver Canucks—then he would become a singer. When he realized he wasn't good enough to play professional hockey, he was determined to have a successful singing career.

About a year after the Big Bamboo contest, Ray and I ran into Michael and another man coming out of a photo shoot near a Greek restaurant on Granville Island.

"Hi Bev, I have a manager now," he said, and introduced us to his uncle Kelly. I was happy for him and told him so, wishing him well in his career.

As I did with all the people Ray and I had dealings with in the entertainment business around town, I had kept Michael's phone number from the Big Bamboo talent show.

A few months after Ray and I bumped into Michael on Granville Island, and five seasons into my PNE job, I called his mom, Amber, and suggested that Michael enter the 1995 PNE youth talent contest for ages thirteen to twenty-one.

She agreed and called Lewis, who was on his fishing boat with Michael. "That lady from the PNE called," she told him, "and said Michael should enter her contest."

Lewis sent Michael home.

Air Canada was one of the sponsors of the PNE youth talent contest, and they would fly me all over B.C. to attend the contests held by community organizations in places such as Nelson, Kelowna, Smithers and Prince George. The smaller communities outside of Vancouver were so happy to have recognition, and they treated me like royalty. They would hold local talent shows, with judges and the whole set-up, and each town would pick a winner to compete in the PNE show. I never interfered with the local choices but had the option to invite an extra contestant if I saw someone I thought was especially talented.

Like everyone else, Michael had to qualify in a preliminary contest, and he ended up competing in New Westminster. But he didn't win. The winner was a guitar player/vocalist. But Michael was so good, singing "All of Me," that I turned to my supervisor, Donna Hunter—who happened to be at the show with me—and said: "I would like to invite him to the PNE. What do you think?"

"He's good, he's good," she said. I told her I was going to invoke my privilege and invite him, and she agreed. I went over to the MC and told him that I was inviting

Michael Bublé to compete at the PNE. Michael's whole family was there for the audition—including Brandee and Crystal—and they were thrilled that even though he hadn't won, he would still be competing at the PNE.

The 1995 fair opened, as it always does, in late August. Michael competed with dozens of other contestants in the youth talent contest and made it to the semifinals, and then the finals.

Hugh, of course, was always a judge, one of five in front of the stage in the Garden Auditorium. Everyone respected his opinion and admired his sense of humour. The other judges would ask to sit next to him, and the parents would sit as close to him as possible. I soon learned that I had to have my assistant cordon him off from the contestants' families, because he would say things out loud that weren't very complimentary. Once, after a not-so-great performance by one contestant, he said, at the top of his voice, "Somebody needs to shoot their parents."

Every day before the show, my assistant filled the judges' glasses with water. One day, Hugh said to me, pursing his lips: "We need to have some vodka in those glasses." I said: "Hugh, it's community entertainment." But the next day I brought in a flask and filled Hugh's glass with water and vodka. I never said a word, but I watched him until he took a drink of his "water." He sipped it, turned to me and tipped the glass in my direction.

When Michael performed in the PNE semifinals, the crowd loved him. And the judges did, too. When the finals rolled around, there were about a dozen contestants left. Two thousand fairgoers crowded into the Garden Auditorium, and when Michael sang "All of Me," the audience went absolutely wild. Afterward, my assistant, who would always gather up the forms from the judges right away so that they couldn't compare notes, tallied the scores.

Michael had won, by a landslide.

The prize was $1,000 and a trip to Memphis to compete in the International Youth Talent Search finals, which included talent contest winners from all over the U.S. and other participating Canadian cities. The Bublés were deliriously happy, and that night, Ray and I joined Michael, his parents and his grandparents for a celebration dinner at Rossini's restaurant in Kitsilano.

Ray, of course, knew talent when he saw it, and even though I wouldn't find out about it from Michael until much later, I was surprised to learn that Ray had gone to Amber and Lewis shortly after the PNE win and said that he wanted to manage Michael. They told him they didn't know what their intentions were for their son at that point, and it never went anywhere. And Ray never once mentioned it to me.

Each year, after the PNE had closed up shop, I would return to my routine of booking the Platters and working on a small project I had created called The Organizer, where I coached corporate- and home-based businesses on a more efficient method of organizing their staff and paperwork. During one hiatus, I did fundraising for the Vancouver Youth Theatre, a respected organization where Vancouver-area youngsters could take acting lessons. I held an acting talent contest for them and raised $30,000 for the theatre.

And, every October, I would accompany the PNE winner to Memphis.

Michael and I arrived on a Thursday and checked into the beautiful Peabody Hotel, famous for the family of ducks that waddled every morning from the elevator through the lobby to the fountain and back again later in the day. The weekend schedule was jam-packed with activities, including a sponsors' reception, a riverboat cruise,

Michael, 20 years old, taken at the Pacific National Exhibition in 1995 after he won the Youth Talent contest, of which I was the coordinator. Michael stands with Jenny Kwan, PNE Board Member and Member of Parliament for Vancouver-Mount Pleasant, and me.

a concert and a trip to Graceland to tour Elvis Presley's home, which for me, felt like the first time each returning trip.

Friday was devoted to rehearsals, with musical directors, a show organizer and guest speakers tutoring contestants about the music business and details such as dress, makeup and stage presence. The singers were given feedback as each performed his or her chosen song. Michael brought the music for "All of Me." During rehearsal, the contestants watched each other perform, and they all thought everyone else was more talented than they were. Michael was no exception. He was worried about the competition, but I would soon learn that he was always worried, always pacing and biting his nails, always doubting his talent, always fretting that he was never good enough.

After rehearsal, everyone went on a paddlewheeler cruise down the Mississippi, and it was magical, with a big barbecue and dance band and wonderful camaraderie among the contestants. Saturday was the final rehearsal, the last preparation for the big show on the Sunday morning.

The finals were held on the Memphis fairgrounds and Michael wore a cream-coloured jacket with dark pants. He was slated to sing in the middle of the lineup, which was chosen randomly, and he did a terrific job, nailing the song and getting a huge reaction from the crowd.

But he lost. Badly. In fact, he didn't even place in the top four, a long way from first prize, which was an audition with Los Angeles agents and a $5,000 cheque.

The judges' comments, which were always posted on

a bulletin board after the contest, noted Michael Bublé was a "Sinatra sound-alike" and "lounge sound-alike." Michael was happy to be compared to Sinatra but utterly devastated at losing.

After the winner was announced—a young girl who sang "Orange Colored Sky"—all the contestants were lined up on the stage and given silver commemorative plates with their names on them. They took a bow, and the curtain closed. But Michael was so upset at losing, at not even placing, that he took his plate and crunched it up like it was a pop can and threw it against the wall. I was standing offstage and told him he did a really good job, but he was disgusted, disappointed and angry, so he just walked away.

That night, we went to a Gladys Knight concert, and on Monday, we flew home.

I knew Michael was still feeling the sting of the loss, but he's such a chatterbox and so focussed that it wasn't long before he was back to his usual self. On the plane, we started talking about what had happened in Memphis, when he turned to me and said: "You know what. Why don't you be my manager?"

"What? What do you need a manager for?"

"I'm going to make this my career, and you know what? I'll give you 15 per cent of everything I make."

I laughed.

"Michael, what's 15 per cent of nothing?"

He threw back his head and laughed loudly.

"I love that. But seriously, I feel you've always been professional, you were always there, but you weren't like a parent, and that's a hard role to play."

And so we became, if somewhat informally, manager and client.

Back in Vancouver, Michael was starting to get noticed by the local press, his win at the PNE attracting lots of attention. He was appearing regularly on local radio shows and getting booked for more singing engagements.

One day, a woman who had been listening to one of the radio stations playing Michael's songs contacted the station and said she wanted Michael to sing at her wedding reception at the Terminal City Club, a posh members-only venue in downtown Vancouver. She was using the Mark Hasselbach Band (Mark has since reverted to his moniker, Gabriel). I knew Gabriel from around town, so when he called me and asked about Michael, I told him that Michael would be a good choice. Like everyone back then, Gabriel could only say: "Who is this kid?" But he hired him. I went with Michael to the reception and waited in the green room while he performed. After the set, Gabriel came in to see me and said: "Yeah, he's great. I can get him lots of work."

And he did, even though Michael hated some of the jobs, like performing with Gabriel's band in the rotunda at the Bentall Centre and in the Sears store in downtown Vancouver at Christmas time, singing carols and wearing a Santa hat. He really didn't like anything that wasn't dignified, anything that wasn't him. "It's not getting me anywhere," he would say.

Even though some of the jobs Gabriel found for Michael were good ones, and Gabriel always paid Michael well, after a while I had to tell him we weren't taking any more of those bookings, because other musicians were calling to book Michael as their front man, and I knew we had to make a change.

Gabriel was okay with that, and when I told Michael that I would be the only one doing his bookings from then on, he was relieved. Gabriel had been a big supporter of Michael's, and they had a great relationship, but Gabriel could be funny about some things. Sometimes, he told Michael to just sing, and not to talk, when they were on stage. One night, Gabriel's sound system went kaput in the middle of a performance, and while he was struggling to fix things, he looked over at Michael, frustrated, and said: "Well, don't just stand there. Say something." Michael said: "Well, you told me never to say anything." I was so amused at the story.

It soon became obvious that Michael needed a musical director, so Hugh introduced me to one of his proteges, a talented local musician named Bryant Olender, who sang and played piano and had been the 1989 youth talent contest winner. It was there he had met Hugh, who had subsequently taken him to Japan to represent Vancouver at a world youth talent showcase. Not only did Bryant perform in Japan, but he ended up being the event's assistant musical director.

Michael tried him out, they clicked and, before long, Bryant was his musical director.

Michael began getting more jobs and played everywhere, at big venues such as Pebble Beach and in Palm Springs, for private functions including Amway conventions in Hawaii, and at the Seattle home of Microsoft boss Bill Gates. And, of course, he played many events in and around Vancouver. On occasion, Dal Richards, a well-known local band leader and musical fixture at the PNE, would invite Michael to perform as a guest with his big band.

Hugh always called Michael and Bryant "the boys." The four of us would get together every once in a while for a big gab session, at Bianco Nero, Hugh's favourite restaurant. He had been a patron for years and had a table in the back, against the wall so that he could always see everyone coming in. He would call me and say, "It's time to get together, so bring the boys."

The four of us would meet for lunch or dinner, and Hugh would order whatever the chef recommended. Hugh always insisted on paying the bill, and we always drank wine and talked and laughed.

Once, we were talking about people who were getting on our nerves, and Hugh told me and the boys that the best thing to do when someone is bothering you is "just turn to them and tell them to fuck off. I do it all the time." We were never surprised by anything Hugh said.

Michael and Bryant were working steadily, and the money was good, the expenses all paid, but Bryant began to want more and one day said to me: "I wish you would recognize that I'm more than just Michael's accompaniment." A few years later, he and Michael had a minor falling out, and Bryant decided it was time to strike out on his own and pursue a solo career.

And I was learning what it meant to "manage" Michael. He was one of those kids who hadn't much liked school, one of those focussed but flighty young men you never pin down. I always wanted to have business meetings with him, so he'd pick me up in his messy red Chevy Cavalier, which was filled with empty water bottles, CD cases and papers, so much junk on the seats and the floor that it was hard to find a place to put your feet. We would go for lunch, but our get-togethers were never long, because he always had to be somewhere else, and he never really wanted to talk about business anyway.

He wasn't the type to go to clubs to socialize, either, preferring instead to hang out with friends, and his girl-friends. Michael always had a girlfriend, and one of the first when I started working with him was Jennifer Lauren, a girl he met at the PNE youth talent search, where she had sung as part of a trio. And, of course, there was Debbie Timuss, his long-time girlfriend in the early years of his career.

As our relationship grew closer, Michael talked to me about almost everything. Although he was close to his sisters and his parents and grandparents, he would confide in me about the things he didn't want to talk to them about. He was young, easygoing and focussed but insecure, always fretting, always worried. Along with his prodigious work ethic and his determination to be the best, he was always so honest about his feelings, so willing to bare his soul.

It was both that strength and vulnerability that came through in his singing, because for Michael, it was all about the music, especially the music of the generations that had come before him, the great crooners like Frank Sinatra, Louis Prima, Bobby Darin and Dean Martin. He talked about them constantly and knew everything about them, every record they made, every concert they headlined, every detail of their lives. "All I want to do," he would say to me, "is get there."

CHAPTER THREE

First Dance

To my grandparents, my parents and family for their love, support and continual belief in me. To Jennifer for her tireless contributions to my charts and compositions. To Beverly, my confidante, my "guardian agent," my friend, for her unending devotion in pursuing my career in every possible way.

*I*f Michael's dedication on his very first CD, which we decided to call *First Dance* and had only six songs on it, had all the charm and sweetness you'd expect from a twenty-one-year-old talent perched on the edge of stardom, it also sent the signal that Michael Bublé, then and now, is all about family and friendships and maintaining the grassroots connections that keep him grounded.

We recorded the CD in 1996, which was turning out to be a big year for Michael. We were still fresh off our trip to the Memphis youth talent show, and it was becoming increasingly clear that Michael's career was starting to take off. He was getting lots of work through the various booking agents around town, including Siegel Entertainment, Lighten Up Productions and Pacific Show Productions.

Many bookings, though, came through MVKA Productions, which was run by Martin van Keken, who bid on and staged events and big conventions all over the world and who often recommended Michael as the entertainment. Martin loved Michael and booked him for events everywhere he could, in Whistler at the convention centre, at the Pan Pacific Hotel in Vancouver, at the Pebble Beach golf club in California and at dozens of hotels and venues around the Pacific Northwest.

I tried to get to as many of the shows as I could but didn't manage to see many of the ones out of town. Ray and I were still booking the Platters, and I was still working at the PNE during fair season, but it was becoming obvious that more and more of my time was being devoted to Michael.

I was still technically acting only informally as his manager, because we didn't have a contract outside of our previous verbal agreement that I would begin guiding his career. All the same, I began booking all his shows and handling all the details, something Michael wanted no part of. He didn't like dealing with anyone except me—the music, to him, was always more important than the details around the music—so I took care of everything, and he would just show up with his band and sing.

It was an arrangement that worked for us.

Michael was always so funny about his shows, because

he was something of a perfectionist when it concerned his singing. He would call me when he was having a bad night and say, "I just suck. These people are driving me crazy, and they're coming up and asking me for requests, and I'm not a request band, Bev, I'm just who I am." But if he was good, if the set was going well, he'd call me and say, "I'm really hot tonight, Bev. Really hot. Really hot."

No matter how the show was going, his stage charm was always on. He intuitively knew how to work the crowd. Conventions weren't his favourite, though, because by the time he got up on the stage, many of those in the audience had already been drinking, and they would feel free to do and say anything they wanted. But he knew how to handle it. If a heckler approached the stage, Michael would just say: "Would you like to come up and sing with me?" and they would back right off. He never got angry, and he was always patient when someone in the crowd was bothering him. He'd just phone me afterward, whenever something didn't go right, and blow off steam about it.

When it came to Michael, my stomach was always in knots, always twirling, because I never knew what he was going to be calling me about. When he was edgy, it made me edgy. Once, his mother, Amber, woke him up—his bedroom was in the basement of the family's house— by smacking him with a pillow. "What are you doing?" he yelled, and swore, because he had been sleeping and didn't know what was going on.

"Bev just told me she's got high blood pressure," said Amber, "and I know it's your fault!"

But he was just like that. He couldn't help himself, and we just accepted it. I used to tell Amber that no matter what was happening with us, I could only imagine how hard it was for Michael, because in so many ways it was like he had no control over his career. His success was as much about timing and luck and the choices we made, choices about venues and shows and songs, as it was about his talent, and we both knew that. But Michael was driven. He never took his eyes off the goal—to become a successful singer—so we just kept going, crossing our fingers that we were heading in the right direction.

Michael made pretty good money in those early days, anywhere from $5,000 to $10,000 a show, which wasn't bad for a local singer in his early twenties who had yet to break into the big time.

And, no matter the take, he was always good about paying his musicians first. Union scale was about $55 an hour, but Michael learned early on that it paid to be generous to the band that has your back. He treated his musicians well and usually gave each of them about $300 or $500 for a night's work. The rest he kept for himself, and at that time, I took very little, because we were just getting established. It really was 15 per cent of nothing.

As word began getting around about this good-looking kid with the velvet pipes, the Burnaby boy with the gift of the croon and an easy, elegant stage presence, the local media also began to take notice, and there were occasional stories in the newspapers and more frequent requests for interviews from radio stations.

One local columnist, Malcolm Parry of *The Vancouver Sun*, was a great supporter of Michael's, always publishing his photo and writing about events where Michael performed, such as a fundraiser for the Greg Moore Foundation in honour of the local Indy race car driver who had died in a fiery crash in 1999. The paper's Kerry Gold also regularly covered Michael's early years on the Vancouver club scene, as part of her duties as the music reporter.

In the meantime, I had been trying to convince Michael's parents that it was time he made a CD. We needed something to give people as a way to promote his talent. They agreed, and I started working on it.

Paul Airey, who had helped with the judging at my PNE youth talent contests, had a recording studio called Avenue Music/Sound Kitchen in town, and when he first saw Michael perform, he told me to call him if we ever wanted help making a CD.

So I did. And he and Michael and I began working on the details. I chose the name of the CD, calling it *First Dance*, because it was his first album and kind of like a first dance, and I just liked it, and they agreed. Of the six songs we chose, there were two originals: "One Step at a Time," written by Ron Irving and David Simmonds, and "Just One More Dance," written by Airey, Ron and Sue Irving and Judy Harnett. There were also four covers, and we had to get permission to use the tracks, which is easier and less expensive than recording the songs live with backup musicians. They were four of Michael's favourites: "Learnin' the Blues," "I've Got You Under My Skin," "I'll Be Seeing You" and, of course, his standby, "All of Me."

It was a lot of fun going to the studio. Before every session, we would all sit around this little room that was like a 1950s diner, complete with candy jars full of jelly beans and Tootsie Rolls. Sometimes Ray would come, and sometimes Amber and Lewis would show up with Michael's grandparents Mitch and Yolanda, and they would bring cheeses and fruit and luncheon meats and biscotti and homemade pizzelles. The boys would talk about hockey and watch a game if one was on. Paul's girlfriend, Judy, would make coffee, but sometimes, the kibitzing would go on too long, and I would say, "Okay boys, it's time to get to work," and they would laugh and get to work.

Because most of the CD was done using the recorded music that we had bought, the sessions went quickly, and we were done after a few weeks.

We pressed *First Dance* at Sunrise Cassette in Richmond, and Kevin Clark took the photograph for the cover, a dreamy shot of Michael that captured his sultry innocence perfectly. Paul charged us a mere $1,000 to make the CD, and we made five hundred copies. Michael's parents happily paid for everything.

I decided that the best way to get the word out, to get Michael some attention from the local press, was to have a CD release party, so I talked to Michael's family and we chose the Cultch, the popular and funky Vancouver East Cultural Centre, a city landmark and long-time hotbed of the arts on the east side.

The party was on December 1, 1996, and we filled the place—it held four hundred—but Amber made sure that all the tickets were sold and then some, and it was elbow to elbow all night. The Cultch people weren't happy because, with all those Bublé fans jostling for breathing room, we were clearly over the venue's limit.

Michael's family was all there, and as they did for every event, they had cooked up a feast—at one point, the whole place smelled like devilled eggs. There was a beautiful carrot cake, too, decorated with a picture of Elvis Presley and the words, Congratulations Michael. Everyone went home with a complimentary bottle of white wine with a *First Dance* label, both the wine and the label made by Michael's family.

And, of course, there was a live band. The drummer was Don Fraser, who had been playing some shows with Michael at the Georgia Bar and Grill, and George McFetridge was on piano. Michael, who always dressed smartly, wore an open-necked shirt and one of his dad's suits, which was cream-coloured and a touch too big, the shoulders swallowing his lean frame. But he looked great and was in fine form. He sang all the songs from the CD, and a few more from his growing repertoire, and the crowd went crazy.

Lisa came up to me at one point and said: "Mom, he's really good. You have to sign him to a legal contract."

We sold three hundred *First Dance* CDs that night, for about $10 each, and even though everyone loved the record, the irony is that Michael didn't, telling me just hours before the event at the Cultch that he was unhappy with it.

"Bev, I hate my CD," he said. "I just don't like it. It's lame. I just didn't see it at the time. It's lousy. I'm lousy. I don't sound good. It's canned music. I hate it."

I probably shouldn't have, but I phoned Paul and told him that Michael hated the CD. But Paul just shrugged it off and said, "Bev, nobody ever likes their first CD, but it usually takes a little longer before they say it."

It was, I was learning, so like Michael to be consumed with insecurity and worry that what he had done just wasn't good enough, even though he was the only one who felt that way.

The *First Dance* party was a huge success and, late in the evening, Michael cornered me and said, "Okay, now will you be my manager?"

I said yes. At the end of the night, after Michael sang and all the thank yous were said, his family called me up onstage and gave me a huge bouquet of red roses. I cried.

"Lucky me," I told them. "Michael picked me. I don't have experience in this area, but we feel good about this. We love each other. And we're going to get in the boat, and we're going down the river together."

His parents and grandparents were thrilled that Michael had asked me, officially, to be his manager, but I told them all that if we were going to do this, we were going to do it my way.

One of Ray's friends was a lawyer, so I asked him to draw up a standard contract. It was eleven pages, with all the detail and wording appropriate for a manager/client relationship. I called Michael and told him the contract was ready, so we agreed to meet at the Yaletown Brewing Company, where Lisa and my future son-in-law, Mike, worked part-time as bartenders.

Michael arrived, wearing a baseball cap turned backwards, sat down and said: "Bev, do you mind? There's a hockey game on," and I just laughed, so he ended up sitting there watching television while I talked to him about our contract.

With Michael, that was just business as usual. He never paid attention to stuff like that, because he always trusted me. So I read the contract to him, I told him what it said, and he said okay. He asked, "Do I need to sign something?" and I said, "Yes, we need a witness." Lisa and Mike weren't working that night, so we asked our server to witness our signatures.

We each signed our copy of the contract, and he took his home. The next morning, he called me.

"Geez, Bevy, I just read through this contract, and the whole thing is for you."

"Well, Michael, that's what it's about. It's a management deal. Of course it's for me. That's why we have the contract. I have to be protected."

It was late December, and as the contract noted, I had a new company, Big Shtick Productions Ltd.

I had given up the company name Del-Carr, renaming it Big Shtick at the prompting of Gabriel Hasselbach, who joked that I always walked softly but carried a big stick. Michael didn't much like it, though, thinking it too slapstick and saying that it didn't suit me, because I was always so positive and could see the good in everything. Years later, I would change the name again, to Silver Lining Management.

The contract was for five years, which took us through to 2001. I was to get the agent rate of 15 per cent of his net earnings, and Michael couldn't do anything without my approval. If he ever made a recording, for instance, I got part of that as well. Most managers take their percentage off the gross, but I never did that. I felt I shouldn't take a percentage of the musicians' fees but only of Michael's cut, because I was his manager, not theirs. It was unorthodox, but I just didn't know any better at the time. Once he understood the details of the contract, Michael was fine with it, because he trusted me, and his parents were happy that we had made it official.

And so it was that Michael Bublé and Beverly Delich started their official relationship as manager and client.

But not everyone in the Vancouver entertainment industry thought Michael had made the right choice.

One night, not long after we had signed the contract, Michael would later tell me, Don Fraser told him: "Michael, I think that was a mistake. She doesn't know anything about the business. You shouldn't have tied yourself up with her for five years."

I didn't know much about the business, that's true, except what I had learned through my work at the PNE and in my business relationship with Ray, but I knew that we would be successful. I intuitively sensed, deep in my bones, that with the combination of Michael's talent and my enthusiasm and persistence, someone would discover us, someone would believe in him like I did.

Don wasn't the only one who gave Michael a hard time about signing with me, but Michael always stood up for me and told anyone who questioned his decision that he wasn't worried, that I would look after him. One local radio personality badgered him, saying, "I'm sure she's a nice lady, but you need to be with an agency in New York." Michael, relating the conversation to me later, simply told him to "shut the fuck up. You don't know anything. I don't see you doing anything that would be any better."

Whatever it was, envy or whatever, we didn't care. We were a team, Michael's family was behind us and we were on our way.

The year got busier and busier. Along with his various bookings and the recording of *First Dance*, Michael had done a commercial for Air Canada and black-tie fund-raisers on the North Shore and for various Variety Club events, including the Cavalcade of Stars for the Burnaby Arts Council. He was also still playing on Saturday nights with the Don Fraser Trio at the Georgia Bar and Grill.

As 1996 was drawing to a close, I got a call from an agency that wanted to hire Michael to entertain at the New Year's Eve after-party at the Pan Pacific for the Three Tenors, Luciano Pavarotti, Plácido Domingo and José Carreras, who were in town performing before a crowd of sixty thousand at B.C. Place Stadium.

The after-party was in a packed ballroom in the hotel, with Pavarotti and his party cordoned off, and we all milled around, eating hors d'oeuvres and chatting, and then Michael took to the stage and sang for some of the world's most famous singers. Pavarotti seemed to like it and told one of his handlers: "Have the boy sing another song," so Michael did just that. Later, during one of his many appearances on the locally shot CBC talk show *The Vicki Gabereau Show*, Michael chatted about how weird the experience was, especially seeing Pavarotti roped off like an exhibit, which he said was like watching "animals in a zoo."

But it marked the beginning of 1997, which would turn out to be an important year for us.

Michael's star was on the rise.

In the spring of 1997, a well-connected Burnaby friend of the Bublés, Sev Morin, called me one day and said he wanted to put on a concert with Michael at the Michael J. Fox Theatre, a lovely little community venue on the grounds of Burnaby South Secondary School, built in honour of another famous Burnaby boy.

Sev had heard about Michael, and during our chat about arrangements for the concert, he told me: "He needs to be in front of David Foster." I told him I didn't know David Foster, the Victoria-born pop music producer who has mentored singers such as Celine Dion and Josh Groban, but Sev said that he did and he was going to try and get an audience. It never happened, but the concert, on April 20, was a huge success. Amber, of course, had worked her social magic and made sure it was sold out. She was so good at filling the six-hundred-plus seats that she even knew who was sitting where and even before the show was telling me who was in what seat. Don was the drummer, again, and one of his backup singers was Jennifer Lauren, Michael's girlfriend.

And then along came *Red Rock Diner*.

It was a musical revue that featured impersonators of famous acts from the 1950s, such as Bobby Darin and Buddy Holly and Elvis Presley. The show was the baby of local DJ legend Red Robinson, and he was staging it with Bill Millerd, the artistic director of the Arts Club Theatre, and creator/director Dean Regan. When they began casting the various parts, a family friend told Michael that he should audition.

I knew it was a good fit for Michael and encouraged him to try out for the Elvis part, but he was hesitant. "Bevy, I can't believe that you think that I can do that kind of stuff. You have to dance and everything." But I knew he could it and that it would be good exposure, a good career move, and I finally convinced him to meet with the casting people and audition for the part.

He did, and then we never heard back.

Not about to give up that easily, I kept calling Bill, from phone booths all over town every time I thought of it. "Bill, I know he can do this," I would say, and Bill would say, "Well, I've seen him at the Georgia Bar and Grill, and he does have a good voice, but I just can't see it; he doesn't dance. I can't see him having this part."

This went on for weeks, and finally, one day when I called Bill yet again, from yet another pay phone, this one on Granville Street, where I was standing in the pouring rain, he said, "All right. Tell him to contact Dean."

Michael started rehearsals on June 6, 1997, and the show previewed on June 27. It opened on July 8 at the Arts Club Granville Island Stage and went on to have a wildly successful, sold-out two-month run.

Robinson was the narrator, and the show, naturally, was about the early days of his career as a Vancouver DJ. The plot revolved around a talent contest featuring the "stars" of the show before they became stars. Michael, dressed as Elvis (though his character was named Val), would come out with an acoustic guitar slung over his chest and do the whole singing and dancing routine to "Jailhouse Rock."

As much as he protested that he couldn't dance, he could, especially after the show held a seven-day dance workshop with instructors to help him and the other performers with their moves. Michael was terrific. The audience loved him and, on most nights, picked him as the winner of the "contest." Michael later shared with me that on opening night, Bill Millerd had announced an "open bar," and Michael assumed that the drinks were free. When he mentioned to Bill that they were charging for drinks, Bill smiled and said: "Michael, I said the bar was open, not an open bar."

The reviews in the local media were laudatory, often

Cast of *Red Rock Diner*, in which Michael played a character based on Elvis. Through the 1997 Vancouver production, Michael would meet and fall in love with Debbie Timuss (kneeling front). They would be together for eight years. JEFF VIMICK PHOTO/*VANCOUVER SUN*

referring to Michael's connection with the audience. One review in the *Province* newspaper noted there was a "ripple in the house" when Bublé came onstage and quoted Dean as saying "This guy's got the makings of a big star."

Red was no less impressed. He sent me a note on November 19, on his letterhead (which said "Red Robinson Management" and had a microphone and floating stars), that expressed what I already knew: "He's on his way to join the company of Mel Tormé, Frank Sinatra, Tony Bennett and Harry Connick Jr.," Red wrote. "His name is Michael Bublé. Remember the name."

I didn't always go to the shows, because Bill didn't want me taking up seats that he could sell tickets for, but I was there on opening night, sitting up front with Paul Airey, who at one point nudged me and said: "Hey, Bruce Allen is sitting behind us."

Everyone knew who Bruce was, the brash and bombastic Vancouver manager, whose client roster over the decades has included musical superstars such as Bryan Adams, Bachman-Turner Overdrive, Jann Arden, Martina McBride and Anne Murray. He was the manager, the guy with the great music industry Rolodex, the guy who knew everyone in the business, who knew how to take raw talent and turn it into superstardom.

And here he was watching Michael. That was good enough for me. I phoned Bruce the next day. I cold-called him, which I knew was a long shot, because people like Bruce Allen didn't just pick up their own phone. But when his office assistant answered, "Bruce Allen Talent,"

I just said: "Is he in?" and, for some reason, she put me right through to him.

"Bruce Allen, you don't know who I am, but my name is Beverly Delich. I saw you in the audience last night at *Red Rock Diner,* and I work with one of the performers in the show and I want to know what you thought of him."

"Who?"

"Michael Bublé."

"You mean the Elvis guy?"

"Yes. What did you think of him?"

"Well, yeah, yeah, he was good, but just a second here. What are you looking for?"

I wasn't prepared for him to ask me that, but the answer came flying out of my mouth.

"Management and a record deal."

There was a pause, and then a chortle: "Just a second. What did you say your name is, because I never want to forget this conversation."

And that was pretty much it. I wasn't even sure what I wanted from him, except some kind of help. I wanted to be Michael's manager, but I needed guidance, too, a co-manager. And Michael and I both knew that there would come a day when I would have to hand him over to someone in the industry who was more qualified than I, someone with more knowledge and more connections.

So I didn't give up. I started calling Bruce's secretary, Terri, every once in a while, trying to wrangle an appointment and pick up our conversation where we'd left off. But I wasn't getting anywhere. Finally, during one of those calls, I asked her: "Am I wasting my time?" and she said, "No, you know, it's just always on Bruce time." Then, one day she called and said I could have fifteen minutes with Bruce. I got in the car, raced down, and when I got there, she took me into his office and said: "Bruce, Beverly," and left us, satisfied that she had done her best.

Bruce came out from behind his desk, shook my hand and invited me to sit with him on the couch. We chatted a bit about Michael, and then I gave him a copy of *First Dance* and asked him to listen to it when he had time. As usual, I spent most of the conversation bragging about Michael and his beautiful voice, telling Bruce that Michael was his own person, that he had that Sinatra sound and was the whole package, and that we just needed someone to help us get him out there.

He looked puzzled.

"I've worked with Bryan Adams and that's rock, and I just don't know what this is. Honestly, I don't know what to do with him, but I will listen to the CD."

I left and expected to hear back from Bruce right away. But he didn't call, at least not soon enough for me, so I was back to bugging Terri, anxious because I wanted her boss's professional opinion about the CD. It took a few days, but he finally called me. He said he had listened to *First Dance* and that Michael had a good voice, but he couldn't help us, because—and here it came again—"I don't know what to do with him."

Michael and I went back to what we had been doing—working hard on bookings, promotion and planning.

That July, Vance Campbell, who managed the Roxy, BaBalu and other popular Vancouver nightclubs for owner Blaine Culling, called me out of the blue. "I understand you manage Michael Bublé, and we hear he's hot and we want him."

It was music to my ears. I called Michael and told him what Vance had said, and he was thrilled, too, because Culling's Granville Entertainment Group was well known in Vancouver. Vance and Blaine wanted to get together with us, so Michael and I met them for dinner at Allegro downtown. We sat in a booth at the back and talked about music. They were friendly and enthusiastic and made it quite clear they wanted Michael for one of their clubs.

There was a slight hitch, they said, but quickly assured us it wouldn't be a problem. At the time of our meeting, a singer named Brian Evans had been performing at BaBalu, a club that featured tapas, cigars and live music that fell somewhere between swing and Miami Latin, á la Desi Arnaz. It was a formula that worked, and BaBalu had become a local hotspot on the corner of Nelson and Granville in the city's entertainment-filled West End.

The hitch was that Vance and Blaine didn't want to renew Brian's contract, which was up that September. They wanted Michael to replace him.

Vancouver is a small town when it comes to the music business, and Michael and I knew Brian by reputation and had already had a business encounter with him. Brian was an American, a cruise ship singer who, while on a stop-over in Vancouver, had popped into the Purple Onion in Gastown on a night when Harry Connick Jr. was a guest performer. I had, coincidentally, previously left a copy of Michael's *First Dance* CD on the desk of the manager of the Purple Onion, and Brian saw it while he was in the club office and later called me.

"I'm holding the CD of a fellow you represent," he said. "I'd like to meet with you guys."

I talked to Michael, and we agreed to meet him. "This is going to be good," I said.

We went to Earl's on Broadway, and Brian started talking, floating the idea that because he was already "well known" around town, Michael would make a great opening act for him, and we could all do really well together. We listened, and then I told him we would get back to him. We left. I just didn't get a good vibe from Brian—neither of us did—so I called him later and told him that his proposal wasn't for us, because Michael was a star in his own right.

But I also knew that one of Brian's strengths was self-promotion, so I called Joy Metcalfe, a society columnist whose gossipy tidbits were a staple in the media. She often wrote about Brian, and I suggested she might want to give as much ink to the local talent as she did for others. She immediately began writing about Michael and talking about him on her radio show.

Vance finally confirmed that they wanted to hire Michael to replace Brian at BaBalu, starting that September, working on Sunday and Monday nights. Michael was still doing *Red Rock Diner*, but the schedule worked out perfectly, because *Red Rock* was dark on those nights, which meant Michael was working seven days a week, at least until *Red Rock Diner* closed.

It was a great break for Michael, and I never missed a night when he was performing at BaBalu. Four little tables were always reserved for me in front of the stage, which amused Vance, because no one in the industry ever did that. Managers and agents usually sat at the back of the house, saving the best seats for the general public, and there were only one hundred or so seats in the club. But I insisted and Vance relented, and I would always fill the tables with friends and people from the music business. Most Sundays and Mondays, Michael's parents and grand-parents would be there, too.

BaBalu did a lot of advertising, so word began to get out about this new kid on the block, and people started lining up for Michael's shows. Often, someone I knew would call me from the lineup and ask me to come and let them in. Michael did a four-hour set, from 9 p.m. to 1 a.m., and he made $1,000 a night, though he didn't pocket much by the time he paid the musicians and his other expenses.

One night, I suggested to Vance that he hold a dance contest at BaBalu. At the time, swing dancing was taking Vancouver by storm, but Vance wasn't sure. It took some doing, but I finally convinced him it would be a great draw for the club. He paid me $100 a week to organize and oversee the contest, which I named "It Don't Mean a Thing If It Ain't Got That Swing." In between sets from Michael and his band, aptly named the Bubble Jets, local dance instructors would give swing dance lessons to the audience while DJ Jason Manning twirled the vinyl and local personality Buzz Bishop served as MC.

I pulled in some of my favourite judges, including Hugh Pickett and various media and entertainment personalities, and the place was packed for the entire eight weeks of the contest. Forty-eight couples entered, and they each paid $25 for the chance to win the $1,200 first prize. Promotional prizes were given out during the intermissions—things like concert tickets and cigars—and the winner was chosen based on applause levels and, of course, the judges' opinions. It was a great time. Everyone dressed the part, and the club was hopping, which made Vance happy.

In fact, things were going so well for us that Michael decided it was time to make another CD, a live recording of his BaBalu show. He wanted it to be live because he loved that Sinatra did live recordings, like his iconic *Live at the Sands*, and he had been so unhappy with the canned music on *First Dance*.

Vance's Granville Entertainment, along with the Bublés, put up the money for the CD, and we hired Turtle Productions, which set up its remote recording truck right on Nelson Street in front of the club. It became a Vancouver event, and the place was filled after BaBalu placed an open invitation in *The Vancouver Sun* earlier in the week: *Hey Daddy-O, Be a part of Recording History when Michael Bublé records his new C.D. "Bublé from BaBalu." It's a Hep Happening as Vancouver's Coolest Crooner puts down some Vibes on Vinyl.*

On November 16 and 17 of 1997, we recorded the live BaBalu shows with Michael and his band.

The CD, which we titled *BaBalu*, had thirteen songs and included a number of classics, including "Mack the Knife," "Can't Help Falling in Love" and "What a Wonderful World." I researched each song—who wrote it and when, and so on—and then contacted the appropriate copyright agency to get the rights. For "Mack the Knife," for instance, I had to find out who owned it, where it was published and where to get the rights, and then I had to contact the Canadian Musical Reproduction Rights Agency, go online and print out a form with all the information for the song and the CD we were making. We paid for each song based on the number of copies of the CD we intended to press, and when we were done, the copyright permissions for the songs on *BaBalu* cost about $1,000.

We mixed the CD at Blue Wave Studios in Vancouver. Amber and Yolanda would bring lunch, sandwiches and homemade biscotti, while the engineers worked on each song, getting it just right. The musicians would come into the studio, too, and each one would take a turn, wanting to fix their part on the record. Finally, Michael said it had to stop, because all the cooks in the kitchen were taking up too much time, and the CD was getting away from what he wanted it to sound like. He and the engineers took control over the final product and worked on it until we all thought it was the way it should be.

The band was pretty much the same group Michael had been playing with since the PNE, and even though circumstances and the variety of his work often meant someone wasn't available and he'd have to find a pinch-hitter, the core band members were usually the same ones who played on *BaBalu*: Ridley Vinson on piano, Danny Parker on acoustic and electric bass, Lou Hoover on drums, Gabriel Hasselbach on trumpet and flute, and Kim Nishikawara on saxophones and flute.

Michael loved the guys in his band—after *First Dance*, he never performed to a canned track again—and they worked well together, but he never really hung out with them, preferring to keep the relationship professional. He wasn't one for partying, or going out after the shows. It was, for him, just about the music.

The *BaBalu* sleeve jacket was done by Hari Singh, who had a pressing plant in his Vancouver basement, and he designed it with me, Amber, Lewis and Michael hanging over his shoulder and asking him to alter this and alter that. The front jacket photograph was a Jonathan Cruz shot taken for *Red Rock Diner*, a smouldering Michael looking out from the shadows, dressed in a black open-necked shirt and a white suit jacket. Its Sinatra-style rat-pack overtones were perfect, right down to the sunglasses sticking out of his suit pocket and the big stogie he was holding in one hand.

For the CD's liner notes, which folded out to three pages, Michael wanted an alphabetical, lower-case listing of everyone he felt he should thank. There were hundreds of mentions that I had to gather from friends, and friends of friends, a long list of family members, musicians, entertainment contacts and journalists. The list started with Paul Airey and ended with Zena's musical staff. It took me forever to alphabetize it.

Among the dedications on the CD, which included thanks to God, his supportive family, his great friends and the media, was a lovely nod to our relationship: *Bev... you are still my guardian angel, and I have as much faith in you as you do in me. I know that together we will realize our goals and dreams!!*

We pressed one thousand copies of *BaBalu*, and, as they had with *First Dance*, his family paid for it all, a bill that came in at about $14,000. The record was finished in the spring of 1998, and Indieland, a Vancouver independent record company, started distributing it. Jim Gordon at Virgin Records was a long-time supporter of Michael's and would often have him come down to the store to perform in the DJ booth. Jim also took some of the CDs to sell in his store, as did a few local independent record shops.

And where there's a CD, of course, there's a CD release party. Or two. Both were held at BaBalu, the first on Sunday, April 26, for the general public, and the second the following night, for family, VIPs and the press. We made invitations, and Amber and I hand-delivered them. Amber drove, I sat up front and, most of the time, Michael was in the back seat, chatting and laughing and snuggling with his then-girlfriend, Karina. The invitation was a CD sleeve that I made and put in an empty case, with a poem inside that I wrote:

> I wonder, you say, have they gone mad?
> A CD case with no disc to be had?
> Read on, my friend, and you will find
> A celebration is planned—one of a kind.
> There'll be appies and toasts
> And a present or two
> Hosted and presented by BaBalu
> Swing by the club April 27th at five
> It will last until seven, lest you're late to arrive.
> It's a CD release and he did it his way,
> Yes, it's none other than the talented Bublé.

There were more than one hundred people at the party, including local luminaries and friends such as retailer

Murray Goldman and politician Grace McCarthy, along
with the usual reporters and personalities from newspaper and broadcast outlets, and everyone got a special
gift made by Amber and Michael's sisters, Crystal and
Brandee. They had melted 45 rpm records and shaped
them into little bowls filled with bubble gum and Tootsie
Rolls, along with a copy of the CD, a cigar with Michael's
headshot as the label, a scrolled biography of Michael, a
book of commemorative matches, Spider-Man candy ciga-
rettes, some tinsel and a Big Shtick business card.

The booze flowed and the food, supplied by Granville
Entertainment, was sumptuous and typical of the day:
chocolate-covered strawberries, veggies and dip, cheese
and fruit platters, chicken satay, an antipasto platter,
spring rolls, mini quiches, baked brie with crackers, corn
and crab fritters with jalapeno sauce, popcorn chicken
with Cajun mayonnaise and prosciutto-wrapped melon.

On a table at the entrance to the party, I placed a
figurine of Michael that I commissioned a friend of my
daughter's to sculpt, for $300. It was him as Elvis, in his
Red Rock Diner role. When Michael saw it, he was ever
tactful and said: "Does that look like me, Bevy?"

"Of course it does."

We would eventually sell ten thousand copies of
BaBalu, an impressive number for a singer who hadn't yet
attracted much attention beyond his hometown.

Michael liked the CD, certainly a lot more than *First
Dance*, but Amber and I loved it, which was no surprise,
because we loved everything he did. Amber would call me
and say that she was housecleaning to Michael's CD, and
she loved it more each time she played it.

Michael posing in 1997 at the club BaBalu with the sculpture I had made for him for his *BaBalu* album release party.

Michael's family and I had been close from the beginning. They treated me as if I was a member of their family, and I felt the same way about them. I would have them over for dinner, and Lewis was always happy that I served hearty food like roast beef, and they always gave me beautiful gifts, jewellery and purses and lovely things, for my birthday and for Christmas.

And they trusted me implicitly with their son. But as time went on, I realized I really didn't have anyone to talk to about Michael, about the personal stuff, and it bothered me. I told Amber that I would love to talk to her about such things, because she was his mom and loved him.

"But I need to know that you can't act like a mom," I told her. "So if I tell you something, you can't act like a mom. You have to act like a confidante."

For instance, I said, if Michael did something bone-headed—like making unfiltered comments to people without thinking first, which he often did—I wanted to be able to discuss it with her without her immediately going to Michael and admonishing him like a mother would.

"Bev," she said, "I promise you that anything you ever tell me will never go to anyone, not even Lewis."

I believed her, and after that, I told her every little thing. And she told me everything, too, about his mood when he left the house, about arguments in their family, about anything that might affect his singing or his career. We kept those conversations to ourselves, and it made our bond even stronger.

The CD was getting good reviews and airtime, Michael was packing them in at BaBalu and I felt that we were really making strides. But his artistic burn was strong, and for every step forward, Michael thought he wasn't where he should be, so impatient was he about moving his career along. Whatever we did, it was never enough for him, so it was my job to encourage him and keep him confident and optimistic. Because as much as his insecurities weighed on me, I just knew, I just always knew, that it would happen for us, for him.

We were always together, always talking, always planning, and Michael, who truly wore his heart on his sleeve, shared almost everything with me. One day, he told me he had fallen for someone in the cast of *Red Rock Diner*.

"There's this girl in the show, and I'm just crazy about her," he said. "And I think she feels it, too. But she's engaged."

Her name was Debbie Timuss, and she was a singer

and a cheerleader in the show, a beautiful brunette. And he had fallen hard. I hadn't met her yet, but I told him, "Michael, don't play games, just sit down with Debbie and ask her if there is a connection."

He did, and she said yes and gave her ring back to her fiancé.

One day, not long after that, I popped into a rehearsal. I was walking down the hallway at the Arts Club and along came Michael, piggybacking Debbie, and they were laughing and teasing each other. The more I watched the two of them together, the more obvious it was. They were so playful and so cute. So much in love.

They would be together for eight years.

CHAPTER FOUR

Singing for
the Prime Minister

With the successful run of *Red Rock Diner* behind us, and the BaBalu shows and CD getting a lot of local attention, it seemed that 1998 might be our year.

It turned out to be anything but.

I was working hard through those months, especially after the *Red Rock* run ended and Michael was only working two days a week. I was scrambling to keep the momentum going, but it seemed that no matter what I was doing, it was never enough. I was his manager, his friend and his confidante, and one of the few people he truly trusted. I talked to him every day, looked after every detail. I calmed his anger, reined him in when he was stressed and was always there to tell him that everything would be all right.

I also did all the paperwork for every event and made sure he showed up at the right place at the right time with the right musicians. If an agency hired him, I would do the contracts, for him and for the musicians. We only ever hired through the musicians' union, because it was important to Michael that we did it that way, that we respected their professional requirements as much as they respected ours.

But with Michael so intent on becoming a big star, it seemed like everything I did seemed to come up short. Oh, he had faith in me, and he appreciated me, but he always wanted more. He would say: "We should be doing this, we should be doing that, I've talked to so and so," and it didn't help that people were always saying things to him, that he would then tell me, like "I shouldn't even be here, I should be way out there."

I used to say to him, "Michael, I'm dancing as fast as I can. I know people come to you all the time and tell you that we should be doing something else, that you should be with someone else. But, Michael, what does that look like?"

And that would usually calm him down. Sometimes, when he was really worried, he talked to his mother about it, and she would say "Michael, Bev is doing her best."

I was. Together, we were charting new ground, and we both knew that. But I had the belief that things would work out, because I've always been a believer. He did, too, only he was so much more impatient about it.

I just knew that it was going to happen.

But Michael, even in the worst of times, and even when he was complaining, always supported the decisions I made for him.

He was discouraged that Bruce Allen hadn't shown

any interest in him, as was I. But one thing I knew and took pride in was that other managers might have moved on when their client's career seemed to stall. Bruce Allen might have moved on; I don't know. But I didn't, and so we stuck together and stuck it out, both of us believing that we would make it, that Michael Bublé would be a star, even while knowing intuitively that the day would come when I would have to hand him over to someone who could take him to the next level, who could make his star shine on the world.

So, for the time being, it was just Michael and me, and all too often my blood pressure was through the roof. When I got off the phone with him after a particularly unsettling conversation, my stomach would churn and my head would feel like exploding.

On a very bright note, Jacqui Cohen, president and CEO of Army & Navy department stores, called Vance and Blaine and asked if Michael and his band would be willing to perform at her Face the World gala on May 30. Every year, Jacqui hosts the feted black-tie gala at her water-front residence. The star-studded evening (Tom Jones and Jackie Collins, close friends of Jacqui's, were there) brings together a very generous group of sponsors, volunteers, friends and patrons, who open up their hearts to help Face the World Foundation continue to improve the lives of those in need. Michael and I were guests at Blaine and Vance's table; the evening was very elegant and Jacqui was the ultimate host.

I was still working at the PNE, and Ray and I were still seeing each other, though we were starting to grow apart. I was so immersed in Michael's career that I didn't have

Michael performed in 1998 for the charitable Vancouver-based foundation, Face the World. ANN HAMILTON/*NORTH SHORE NEWS*

time for anything else, and I could sense that Ray was beginning to resent it, that he felt left behind.

Michael, thankfully, was still working at BaBalu. One night, in late spring of 1998, I was in the club when Vance came up to me and said he had some bad news, that he'd had a meeting with Blaine, who was upset because no one was drinking on Sunday and Monday nights at the club, Michael's nights, because the next days were working days. They were just coming to hear Michael sing, and the club wasn't making any money.

They had to let Michael go.

Vance said he felt sick about it and didn't agree with Blaine and told him that he was making a big mistake, but there was nothing he could do. He gave us two weeks' notice, and Michael played his last performance at BaBalu on May 31, 1998.

To be honest, Michael was okay with the decision, even though the musicians hated losing the regular work. He was only making $1,000 a night, and he had to pay the musicians and his expenses out of that, so he had little left. And he had done pretty much everything he could at the club. The CD had done well as an independent issue, but BaBalu had run its course.

But I also knew that it would be another reason for him to be upset, not only because I didn't have any long-term answers for him about where we were going, but worse than that, I didn't have anything else immediately lined up.

So I called the manager of the Purple Onion and made an appointment to see him, thinking the club would jump at the chance to have Michael. And they did.

At the time, the club switched up its music every night, so they booked Michael for Tuesdays and Wednesdays only. The deal was $500 a night and whatever we got from the door, but of course, the musicians' pay came out of that, and there wasn't much left once the expenses were settled up.

It was an awful decision. We didn't know until we started there that the Onion wasn't the Vancouver hot spot it had once been. No one came, and we stayed only a few weeks over the summer.

I knew this would set Michael off again, so I started scrambling to find something.

And, once again, Bill Millerd rode to our rescue, his phone call coming like a serendipitous bolt out of the blue.

The Arts Club was staging a new show called *Swing*, about the big band era of the 1940s, when musicians such as Duke Ellington, Lionel Hampton and Louis Armstrong played in local clubs around town. They wanted Michael to help them recreate the Vancouver era when swing was king.

The show, Millerd said, was part of the lineup to inaugurate the reopening of the Stanley Theatre, a small historic venue on Granville Street that had been the focus of a four-year, $9-million restoration campaign, much of it coming through fundraising from locals committed to saving the venerable venue from the wrecker's ball. It had been restored and would be devoted to live local enter-tainment, presenting plays, musicals and revues.

Debbie was also hired to perform in *Swing*, and after Michael's success in *Red Rock Diner* (and *BaBalu* making a splash in the Top 10 Independent list at HMV), I couldn't resist asking Bill, "Is he going to be the star?" knowing full well that the Arts Club was far too egalitarian to have a star system in its shows. I understood—it was community theatre, after all—but I liked to tease him.

Swing was a good production, and it was a hit. Michael's big song was "Begin the Beguine," but it wasn't like *Red Rock Diner*, where he had been the unofficial star. This show focussed far more attention on the band and the music, on the Tommy Vickers Orchestra and bandleader Gary Guthman, than on the singers.

The show ran from October 28 through the end of the year, and Michael made $1,000 a week, but when it ended, he was ready to move on.

If there was a bright spot in the midst of all this, it was a personal one: Lisa and Mike got married in September at the Unitarian Church on Oak Street, which had once been the home of Temple Sholom. It was a lovely wedding, and I sang "Sim Shalom" while the newlyweds signed their papers after the ceremony. The reception was at the Westin Bayshore, and it was quite the party. Gabriel Hasselbach's band provided the music, and there was lots of singing and dancing, including plenty of traditional Jewish music and horas. The Bublés were all there, and Michael got up onstage with the band and serenaded the couple.

I was so happy for Lisa and happy, too, to have Mike Bishop as my son-in-law.

After *Swing*, Michael was still doing occasional performances around town, including a New Year's Eve benefit at the H.R. MacMillan Space Centre at the Vancouver planetarium, but, as 1998 turned into 1999, I prayed that things would pick up for us.

And they seemed to.

That spring, Michael got his first taste of Hollywood, when he was tapped to do a cameo singing "Strangers in the Night" in *Duets*, a film about a professional karaoke hustler who reconnects with his daughter, starring Gwyneth Paltrow, Paul Giamatti and Huey Lewis. The movie was partially shot in Vancouver but was a box office flop, and although the experience was good, Michael's song wasn't included on the soundtrack.

Meanwhile, I continued to follow every lead that we got, no matter how odd or trivial it seemed at first.

At one of Michael's appearances around town, as often happened, someone had given him a business card, with a suggestion that he get in touch with a Las Vegas entertainment mover and shaker named Steve Paled, who might be able to help with his career plans.

I called Steve.

It turned out that he was going through a breakup and asked me to call him back in a week or so. When I did, and told him that we had been referred by a friend of his who had seen Michael perform, Steve said, "Who is this kid?" and I told him all about Michael. He listened, and then suggested I call a friend of his in New York named Mike Cutino, who owned a New York entertainment magazine and had plenty of industry contacts in New York and Las Vegas, people like Steve Wynn, who owned the Bellagio.

I called Mike Cutino, and he said he was interested in our story and in Michael, but he wanted us to come to New York. He said that he wanted to get involved and that he had plenty of connections, but I wanted to be up front and make sure that both he and I were protected should anything come of his efforts. I went to a lawyer and spent $3,000 drafting a contract that stipulated that any money Michael made through Mike's contacts would result in a 15 per cent commission to Mike Cutino's company.

I never felt that Mike Cutino was going to take advantage of me, though, or of Michael. Whenever we talked about money, he would always say: "Just buy me a coffee and a doughnut."

Michael and I, not knowing where this lead would take us, flew to New York. Mike met us at the airport, and drove us to the Roosevelt Hotel. Steve had flown in from Las Vegas, and the two of them wined and dined us. They took us to the Mickey Mantle restaurant and all the local Jewish delis. We explored Central Park and talked about music, and I could tell the two of them loved Michael and saw in him the promise that I did.

Mike arranged for Michael to be the cover story on the September issue of his *New York Nightlife* magazine, which was a huge boost for us, and Michael also performed at a little New York club. I had mentioned to Mike, before we even went to New York, that I was hoping he could get us into the William Morris Agency, which was one of the biggest and best in the business, but he said he didn't know if he could.

Turns out he could.

Michael and I, along with Steve and Mike, went to the William Morris office and met with one of the agents. The five of us went out to lunch, sat at a big table and talked about Michael. The agent treated us with such respect, and it felt great, as if we were the centre of the entertainment universe at that moment. When lunch was over, we left with nothing more than a commitment that the firm would give us some consideration, and we headed back to the agency. Michael was walking with the William Morris agent ahead of Steve, Mike and me. Steve turned to me and said: "He's just totally Elvis, isn't he. So cute."

The next day, Michael and I were sitting in the lobby of the Roosevelt, waiting for our cab to take us to the airport. Although we had really accomplished nothing concrete in terms of moving his career forward, it didn't feel that way. It felt like someone important had finally taken notice.

Michael turned to me: "Things are good with us, aren't they."

It wasn't a question, it was a statement.

A few days after we returned to Vancouver, I phoned the William Morris agent.

"Beverly," he said, "it was so nice meeting you. Michael's darling, and he does have a really good voice. But we don't know what to do with him, because he doesn't have a professional CD with a label that we can promote; he doesn't have a show or a tour. I just wish you all the best and hope that someday we will be able to do something with him."

It was March 1999, and it was, by now, a familiar refrain.

After that disappointing news from William Morris, I was feeling low. Michael was making a decent living doing live theatre, but I knew it wasn't enough to take him where he needed to go with his career. One morning, while I was

Despite Bublé's boyish charm and brilliant vocals, achieving success wasn't easy. DAVID CLARK/*THE PROVINCE*

sitting at the dining room table having coffee with Lisa, I began to cry. I told her that I was worried and didn't know what else to do with him.

"Mom," she said, "do you really still think he has that certain something, and should you even keep trying?"

But I didn't even hesitate: "Does the sun keep coming up in the morning?" I said. And I meant it.

So I decided to go to Las Vegas and see if I could get Michael some bookings, singing in hotel lounges. I knew it was a long shot, but it was worth a try. I phoned the Luxor, the Rio, the Bellagio and several other hotels, got the names of the entertainment coordinators and then phoned Amber. "Pack your suitcase," I said, "because we're going to Vegas."

I put some promotional kits together, which included Michael's bio and *BaBalu* CDs, and off we went. I had made reservations at the Luxor, and we spent three nights there. Getting in to see the entertainment directors was no easy task, but I phoned each one, told them I was an entertainment coordinator at the Pacific National Exhibition in Vancouver and wanted to talk to them about an artist I represented. They were all non-committal, and not one of them would give me an appointment, instead suggesting that I just come by and drop off the promotional information.

Amber and I did so much walking that we got blisters on our feet. At one point, a loud jet roared overhead and Amber looked up and said jokingly: "Look, your son is flying my son." We laughed, because Daniel was just graduating from Embry-Riddle Aeronautical University in Arizona, with a degree in aerospace studies, and working on his commercial pilot's licence. Little did we know that several years later, Daniel would call me before one of his Learjet flights and say: "Guess who I'm flying today, Mom? Michael Bublé." Or that he would one day be flying Paul Anka, who would become such a big part of Michael's success that when my son introduced himself, Paul would shake his hand and say: "You're Beverly

Delich's son? Beverly Delich is your mother? You have a lovely mother."

From a professional perspective, our foray to Vegas was a bust—we didn't land Michael any work—but Amber and I had a lot of fun, and we got to know each other even more. We played the slots, hit the buffets and shopped. We talked about our lives, and she would say: "Bev, I can't believe all the things you have done. I got married, had three kids and here I am. You definitely need to write a book!" It was, despite our failure at getting Michael some exposure, a good trip.

And then, out of the blue, in June 1999, I got a call asking if Michael would perform at a private function at the Pebble Beach golf resort in California.

Those kinds of bookings were gold, because a rep would call, ask how much, I would say $5,000 and they would cover everything else, all the expenses on top of the fee. I went down with him on this trip, along with all his musicians.

The boys, of course, wanted to play golf once we got there and kept bugging me to get them on the course. I just laughed and said, "Who do you think I am, Houdini? You can't just play Pebble Beach."

It was a great event, though, first class all the way. We had lunch the day of the performance and Michael hit the buffet, which was fantastic, with all kinds of seafood. Michael loved raw oysters, and he kept going back and getting more, bringing plate after plate back to our table. The boys were all telling him to stop, and I did, too, and he just laughed and said: "Bevy, I could eat these all day. I never get sick."

And he didn't. Until after the performance. And then he was sicker than a dog.

Back home, Michael did a return engagement in *Swing* at the Stanley Theatre, in the last two weeks of August.

And then along came another movie.

Rob Merilees, a friend of Michael's, was working with a partner producing *Here's to Life*, a film that was shooting in Victoria with Eric McCormack of *Will & Grace* and the venerable James Whitmore.

The producers wanted Michael to sing five songs for the movie's soundtrack, including "When You're Smiling" from *BaBalu*, and two original songs, "Dumb Ol' Heart," which Michael wrote, and "I've Never Been in Love Before," which Michael had written with Bryant. Although Michael couldn't technically write music, he was an innately gifted lyricist and could sit down at a piano and work with a musician until they came up with the song that was just the way he heard it in his own head.

Sometime after the movie was released, Rob wanted to produce a CD of Michael's songs from the film. I panicked, because there was nothing stopping him from doing it and making money from it. But I was so worried that Michael would be furious, and I told Rob so. I think that because he was Michael's friend, he respected my wishes, and I was always so grateful that he never produced the CD.

As the year wound down, Amber and I decided we needed to have a New Year's Eve party, a millennium bash that we called the Party of the Century, so I called various venues and booked a ballroom at the Delta Vancouver Airport Hotel in Richmond.

We knew we could sell it out, especially with Amber

in charge of ticket sales. Tickets were $150 each, with a champagne toast at midnight. We selected a menu, but we didn't ask for samples in advance, and on the night of the party, Amber was disappointed. Being Italian, food was everything to their family and something they took great pride in. The dinner wasn't like anything she would have served, and there wasn't enough of it, even with five courses that included steak, chicken and salmon, as well as ice wine sorbet and lemon poached shrimp. She was mortified that the guests weren't getting fed as well as they would have if she and Yolanda had catered it.

Debbie was there, and the band, and Michael sang all his favourites. He pulled me up onstage to join him in "Auld Lang Syne," and it was a great celebration.

But it was also the start of a brand new year.

In late January 2000, Michael and a sixteen-piece band opened for Dionne Warwick at a gala benefit at the Vogue, for the Vogue Theatre Restoration Society, another group of committed Vancouver art patrons who were raising funds to rehab the cherished venue on Vancouver's theatre row. Warwick was sick, performed in a cracking voice and, to everyone's disappointment, didn't show up for the after-party. One newspaper review noted that Warwick's opening act, Michael Bublé, had "hammed it up a little too much during his brief set... Bublé, though, can be forgiven the cheesiness thanks to his velvet pipes and irrepressible cuteness."

We decided it was time to launch a website. It would be another way to get the word out about Michael, about *BaBalu*, about what he had been up to and what was coming.

I contacted Scott Smith, who with his wife Shannon had a Vancouver website design company called ss Media, and the four of us met a few times and hashed out the details of what the site would look like and what would be on it. It had to be classy and stylish, with a retro yet modern lounge feel, and the Smiths came up with something Michael and I both liked for Bublé.com.

The content included a biography, photographs, audio clips and a list of when and where Michael was performing. One of their clever ideas was to get Michael to write his signature, which they reproduced on the site and helped bring some of his personality into play. We didn't have much money, of course, so the Smiths graciously let us pay the $3,000 bill over several months. They maintained the site for the next few years, and later, when Michael signed with Warner Bros., they worked for a time with the record company.

There had been talk, meanwhile, that *Swing* would be revamped into a show called *Forever Swing* and begin an eastern tour, starting in Toronto in the spring of 2000, before going on the road in the U.S. Dean Regan was putting it together for the U.S. company that had bought the rights, and we were thrilled when it was given the green light, especially when Dean decided to hire Michael, and most of the original *Swing* cast, including Debbie, for the tour.

It was something to look forward to, and I saw it as another turning point.

I knew there would be rehearsals and that he would find it difficult to work in Toronto when his life was back in Vancouver, so one day I said: "Michael, instead of just going to Toronto, you need to move there."

"What? Move? Why?"

I told him I didn't want him to end up like many other local talents who could never break into the big time because they never left home, that if he didn't he would just be somebody who went on tour and came back again.

The truth is, I felt that we had accomplished everything we could in Vancouver and that it was time to move on, to take a chance.

Michael had been to Toronto before, for other one-off performances, and after giving it some thought, he agreed that it was a good idea. He and Debbie rented a Toronto apartment and went into rehearsals. *Forever Swing* was set to open March 31, 2000.

I went to Toronto for a visit in mid-March, after my friend Duff MacDonald invited me to come and see him in the production of *Godspell* that was playing there. I was only there for a few days, and it was freezing cold, but I saw some friends and was happy to spend some time with Michael and Debbie.

Back home, it wasn't long before I started hearing some grumbles from Michael. As always, he would call me every day, because he liked to talk, to keep me updated. But he kept telling me that he was meeting people who were asking him who his manager was and why he wasn't represented in Toronto and why he didn't go on local shows and that he needed more exposure.

As usual, that kind of discussion with Michael made my insides churn.

It didn't help that I had recently had another brief

meeting with Bruce Allen, updating him on what Michael had been doing, relating that there had been an interest in his career from other industry people and reiterating that we really needed help in ensuring that Michael was headed in the right direction. But once again, Bruce just listened and didn't say much. It was disheartening.

I had also put in a call to Terry McBride at the Nettwerk Music Group, a Vancouver record company that managed acts such as the Barenaked Ladies and Sarah McLachlan. Terry was very nice, and knew who Michael was, but said he felt there was nothing they could do for us at that point in Michael's career, because we didn't have what managers at his level considered a professional CD that they could use to promote him.

The CD, once again, was the calling card.

That June, with me still in Vancouver and Michael in Toronto, I got a call: Michael was invited to sing at a private function at the Seattle home of Microsoft boss Bill Gates and his wife, Melinda. We were beyond excited, because even though it was low-key, we knew there would be many high-powered people there. Michael flew to Vancouver and decided to drive down. He picked up Bryant, who was to be his pianist at the event, early in the morning, and the two headed south across the border for the late afternoon performance.

The Gates's house was by then famous not only because of its owner but because of its size and its state-of-the-art technology. The location was so guarded that Michael and Bryant weren't even given an address. They had instructions to go through a series of checkpoints, where they were to receive further instructions. When they hit Seattle, they headed toward Lake Washington and the first checkpoint in the suburb of Medina. A security guard on the side of the road directed them to the second checkpoint, where they were told to head down a winding driveway toward the water. The house was built into the hillside, and the stage was set up in the front yard, right on the waterfront. The evening was a fundraiser for the University of Washington, and rumour had it that the guests had anted up $100,000 each.

By the time the boys arrived, the caterers were already setting up the tables, so Michael and Bryant started setting up their gear as well. They were surprised and delighted when Bill came by to say hello and to thank them for being part of the event. Then they had a few hours to kill before showtime and retreated to relax in a little guest house on the grounds that had been reserved for the band. It was full of computers like nothing they had ever seen, all of the monitors encased in hardwood frames. And there was food, quite a spread.

It was a memorable night. Michael sang and Bryant played, and the guests dined and danced—Michael even invited the host and hostess to take the floor for a special dance of their own—while the sun set over the water.

Back in Vancouver, Michael stayed long enough to attend the July screening of *Here's to Life* at the Ridge Theatre before heading back to Toronto.

With not much happening in Vancouver, and with Michael clearly needing my help back east, I decided to move to Toronto. My family and friends were a bit surprised, but no one really questioned my decision. I would go in September, right after the PNE.

I had worked for eleven seasons at the fair but felt I had done all I could there, and my heart just wasn't in it. I gave my notice. It was sad and a bit scary, because I really didn't know what would happen with Michael in Toronto, much less beyond that.

As always, Michael's work ethic was strong, and even when times were relatively lean, he was still juggling several jobs. In Toronto, along with *Forever Swing*, he was singing Friday nights at the Reservoir Lounge. He had been told that the Reservoir was the hip place to perform in town, and it did give him great exposure, which was good because it didn't pay much.

My last day at the PNE was hard. I was excited to be going to Toronto, but I knew that I would miss everyone and the work that I had loved doing. I had made so many close friends during that time, friends that would remain my friends forever. I remembered that, eleven years before, our little talent contest had started outside on a small stage on the midway, in the pouring rain. Hugh Pickett had complained that it was pathetic, and he was right, so they moved it into the Rollerland building, beside the beer garden. When the turnout for the show proved to be bigger than they expected, they moved us to the lagoon stage and then into the Garden Auditorium. We had taken that little talent contest a long way, and I was leaving with much pride in all that I had accomplished.

My bosses had a surprise for me after the final talent show. They asked me to come up onstage, while the audience was still there, and told the story about how I was moving to Toronto to manage Michael Bublé, and then presented me with two wonderful gifts, a little gold Ferris wheel pin and a painting of the fair.

It was lovely, and bittersweet, but I knew it was time to move on. I was taken aback, though, when band leader Dal Richards had the nerve to announce from the stage one day during the fair that Michael Bublé had moved to Toronto, and "we wish him lots of luck because now his career can move on, and he can be with agents who can make a difference."

My family supported my move to Toronto, as did Amber and Lewis, so I knew I was making the right decision. With my final season of the PNE behind me, I put my stuff in storage, Lisa and her husband, Mike, moved into my apartment on Fourth Avenue and, right after Labour Day in 2000, I flew to Toronto.

I rented a little apartment downtown. The days were very long, though, because there really wasn't anything to do. I knew that Michael was a little shocked that I had actually pulled up stakes and made the move, but he told me he was happy that I was there.

He had become chummy with a local radio personality, Jaymz Bee, who worked at JAZZ FM and was a musician in his own right, with a fourteen-piece band called the Royal Jelly Orchestra. Michael had met Jaymz in Vancouver, when he was in town checking out the jazz scene and had dropped in for a performance of *Swing*. When Michael moved to Toronto, they became buddies. They hung out, played Frisbee and tennis, went sailing and worked out together at the gym. Michael was always on his radio show, and Jaymz had introduced him to the owner of the

Reservoir Lounge, and the two of them even performed together around town, including at Toronto's iconic Royal York Hotel.

In the months before I moved to Toronto, Jaymz was one of the people who had been bugging Michael about his "absent" manager. Michael would tell him: "Wait until you meet her. She's a really classy lady and very professional."

When Jaymz and I finally met, he said it was a pleasure to meet me, because he didn't think I was real. Michael, who was always adept at making me feel good, said: "You know, Bev, it doesn't matter who you are, just so I have a manager. But it just so happens that you're classy as well. You're a good businesswoman and people take you seriously."

By the time I settled in Toronto, *Forever Swing* had closed, in preparation for the U.S. tour, and Michael didn't have much to do, except for the Reservoir Lounge job. I would go on the nights he performed, just like I did when he was at BaBalu, and order him a pizza before he started the show.

One night, eating his pizza, he said: "You know what's wrong with you? You are blinded by love. You love me so much that you can't see that I will never get anywhere or amount to anything."

I looked at him.

"Michael, I do love you, but I am not blinded by love. You are talented, and I believe with all my heart that we will realize our dreams."

But it was a tough time. I would send out packages to the local entertainment agencies and call them up, trying to get him jobs, but it was September and everything was already booked, and in many cases, the agencies preferred to hire their local entertainers first.

Michael, once again, was not happy with his career, but we carried on, because that's all we knew to do.

On September 9, we went to the Toronto International Film Festival premiere of *Duets*. Michael's part in the movie was so minor, and we really weren't on the radar, so when we got to the theatre, nobody knew who we were or where we were supposed to be standing or sitting. So we hung around outside the theatre, and Michael was getting more agitated. Gwyneth Paltrow passed right by us on the red carpet, and I was getting increasingly flustered and Michael was ready for a meltdown, when a man came up and introduced himself to me.

It was Michael McSweeney, a Toronto businessman who knew everyone in town and was always at the big social events. He had seen Michael and Debbie in *Forever Swing* and had previously hired them, along with comedian Mary Walsh, to perform at the annual general meeting for the company he worked for. After the event, Michael stayed behind and performed for some of the VIPs, and when he was packing up, McSweeney told him that he was connected and that if he could ever help, he'd be happy. Michael demurred but then changed his mind and followed him onto the escalator, handing him a newspaper article and a *BaBalu* CD, which he told him to use as a coaster if he didn't like it.

McSweeney sent the CD to former Canadian prime minister Brian Mulroney. He had been Mulroney's executive assistant in the mid-1980s, and they remained close friends. The Mulroneys' daughter, Caroline, was getting married in Montreal later that fall, and Michael told them that this young singing sensation would be perfect to entertain at the reception.

When he approached us on the red carpet, Michael introduced us, and then Michael McSweeney said: "Come with me and I'll show you where we can sit."

He arranged everything and we went right in, and afterward he asked us to join him and his wife, Heidi, for a drink. I don't know what it was about him, but I felt so comfortable that I started to pour my heart out, telling him that we were lost in Toronto, that nothing was working out for us and that Michael, who was sitting there biting his nails as always, was upset that things were not going as we had hoped.

He said: "Let me see what I can do for you."

He was so plugged in, and he and Heidi had such big hearts, always inviting Michael and me over for dinner, always encouraging Michael about his singing and his future, and praising me for the work I was doing with Michael.

McSweeney was also urging the Mulroneys to hire Michael because he knew that renowned music producer David Foster was going to be a guest at the nuptials. It worked: Brian wanted to hear him in person first, though, so McSweeney drove Michael to Montreal and they were soon having dinner with Brian, Mila and Caroline. Brian, fancying himself a singer, got up and sang "Paper Doll" with Michael, and then offered him the job that would change everything: to sing at Caroline Mulroney's wedding reception at the Windsor Hotel, as part of her star-studded September 16 nuptials to New Yorker Andrew Lapham.

At the reception, with David and the former prime minister standing on the sidelines, Michael and a seventeen-piece band performed half a dozen songs, including "What a Wonderful World," "Can't Help Falling in Love," "Dumb Ol' Heart" and "Mack the Knife." Afterward, he was sitting at a table with David and the McSweeneys, when Mulroney came over, took David in a headlock and said: "You've got to do something with this kid."

And David said, in that disheartening refrain that had become so familiar to Michael and me, "What'll I do with him?"

And Michael, my Michael, who couldn't help himself, said: "If you don't know what to do with me, who does?"

The next day, Michael headed to Le Jardin at the Ritz-Carlton and performed again for the Mulroneys, this time at a private reception, and before he was done, both Brian and his son, Ben, were up onstage singing duets with him.

The McSweeneys' support for Michael didn't end there. They were soon working with David to get bookings for Michael, who performed for the next few years at various fundraisers and private functions in the U.S. and Canada, singing for business titans Paul and Jacqueline Desmarais and Hilary and Galen Weston, and, years later, in 2004 in Palm Beach, for Mulroney's sixty-fifth birthday party.

In the meantime, to make ends meet in Toronto, I was not only doing a little vocal training, but in November I also got a job as a telemarketer for Sitel, selling packages for cable television. I didn't have any choice, because I just couldn't sit around. I needed some income. Michael wasn't working that much, so I took the training, six weeks of it. The office was right across the street from my apartment building, so it was perfect. But I hated the Toronto

Eventually, Michael was noticed by world-renowned music producer David Foster at an unlikely gig—the wedding of former Canadian prime minister Brian Mulroney's daughter in September 2000. WAYNE LEIDENFROST PHOTO/*THE PROVINCE*

weather, which was just so cold and something I wasn't used to.

I know Michael felt bad that I had to go to work, so I didn't tell him that I was doing telemarketing. I told him instead that I was doing market research, because I didn't want to make him feel any worse.

And then *Forever Swing* called and said the show was continuing and they wanted him to go on tour. It would start at the end of December and would last through the spring of 2001, with stops in Victoria; Baltimore; Detroit; Toronto; Chicago; Washington, D.C.; Richmond and Norfolk, Virginia; Philadelphia; Las Vegas; and Montreal.

The tide seemed to be turning.

Not only had Michael received two Genie Award nominations for the songs he wrote for *Here's to Life*, but David Foster, clearly impressed with Michael's wedding singer turn (ironic, because Michael always said that, at times, he felt he was nothing more than a wedding singer), and perhaps taking the former prime minister's words to heart, was starting to show more interest in Michael.

As he did for all the acts he took under his wing, David liked to test them out on the public. He began flying Michael to Los Angeles for various functions, such as the Carousel of Hope in Beverly Hills, a huge fundraiser for juvenile diabetes that attracted dozens of Hollywood's biggest stars.

I had made the arrangements for Michael to go to Los Angeles, but the day before the event, I got a phone call from David's assistant asking where Michael was. They were waiting for him at the rehearsal and wondered why he hadn't shown. I had got the date wrong. I called

Michael, who wasn't happy, but he was always forgiving, so we scrambled and managed to get him on the next flight out later that day, flying first class.

The Carousel of Hope was a grand fundraising ball for the Barbara Davis Center for Diabetes, and it was held on October 28 at the Beverly Hilton Hotel. It was billed as the "world's premier charity event," and anybody who was anybody in Hollywood was on the guest list, including Dustin Hoffman, Goldie Hawn, Jackie Collins, Kevin Costner, Pierce Brosnan, Sidney Poitier, Raquel Welch, Merv Griffin and Aaron Spelling. Michael Jackson arrived, wearing an elaborate gold suit with a matching waistcoat and tie, accompanied by Dame Elizabeth Taylor.

It was Hollywood royalty, and Michael, I knew, would be star-struck.

I had stayed behind in Toronto but wasn't surprised when the phone rang at 2 a.m., my time, on the night of the event.

Michael was over the moon.

"Bev, you can't believe it. Bev, everyone knows David. Everyone, Bev. You can't believe it. He doesn't even have to move, people just keep coming up to him. And Bev, everyone's here. Bev, I met Liz Taylor. Bev, I met Michael Jackson. Bev, you can't believe it."

I, of course, phoned and woke up Amber and related the whole conversation, and she was just as excited as we were.

And then, one day not long after that event, David called me and, in that forceful plain-spoken way he has, said: "You need to move back to Vancouver." He said the three-hour time difference between Toronto and Los

Angeles, not to mention the geographical divide, just wasn't working.

I was never so happy. I hated the weather in Toronto, I missed Vancouver and I really missed my family. I gave notice at my apartment, rented a place in Vancouver and was never more relieved than when I got on that plane in Toronto on Christmas Day and headed home, the snow falling behind me.

With David in our corner, and Michael going on tour in *Forever Swing*, the first year of the new millennium was ending on a high note.

CHAPTER FIVE

Beverly, This Is Paul Anka

*I*t was good to be home, to leave Toronto behind and look ahead to what 2001 would bring.

I was back in my old building in False Creek, having rented a little one-bedroom apartment right underneath my old one, which Mike and Lisa had taken over when I went to Toronto and where they were happy to stay with my blessing. Michael and Debbie stayed in Toronto, preparing for the *Forever Swing* tour.

I reconnected with old friends, including Ray, though we were no longer a couple, and I began doing vocal coaching again. I first started teaching voice in 1998, between contracts at the PNE, and did a bit of coaching in Toronto, so when I returned to Vancouver, I picked up where I had left off.

To attract vocal clients, I had put an ad in the *Georgia Straight*, a free weekly newspaper distributed all over

Metro Vancouver. My marketing line was: "Learn to sing and perform and have fun doing it." The phone started ringing, and I always interviewed applicants in advance, because I wanted to be sure they had some talent. It was all a cappella, without accompanying music, and the clients would come to my place. I really loved it. People would sometimes ask if I ever coached Michael, and I would just laugh.

Michael and Debbie came out to Victoria in mid-January for a week-long run of *Forever Swing*, and of course, we all went over to see him. But then they went right back to Toronto to start the eleven-city tour that would take them through the end of March.

No matter where he was, though, Michael and I still talked or emailed each other every day—he had a cell phone and a little laptop—but in the three months he was on tour, not much else was happening with his career, and we didn't know what he would be doing next. He was, again, making $1,000 a week, which was decent money, and he insisted I take a commission, and so I did, the first time I had officially done that.

When he called me from the road, we would chat about the cities he was in, the show and how things were going, and I knew that although he was happy to be working, his heart wasn't in it.

In the six years we had been together, Michael's career had always been a roller coaster ride, a ride with so many highs and lows that at times it was dizzying. Michael always felt he was stuck in the valley, never at the peak, even though Amber and I thought there were many highs, such as *Red Rock Diner*, singing at the

Babalu Nightclub, *Forever Swing* and singing for Bill Gates.

But for Michael, the only high was going to be a recording contract.

And even though he would complain that he wasn't where he wanted to be, and even though we both knew that, as his manager, I could only take him so far, Michael always treated me with respect. He would get frustrated and sometimes angry, but he was always a gentleman, driven but courtly, which was an unusual trait, a dichotomy in many ways, for an ambitious twenty-five-year-old.

Amber always said that Michael never treated anyone in his life as well as he treated me. I often wondered if that would have been true had I been a man and not an older woman. But I never questioned it and neither, it seemed, did Michael.

I was doing everything I could, with all my heart.

In the course of many conversations Michael had with David Foster, David suggested that we contact his friend, music producer Bruce Roberts, who "has the longest arms in the industry" and had worked with Barbra Streisand, Cher, Celine Dion, Patti LaBelle and Dolly Parton.

With Michael still on tour, I did just that, telling Bruce that we had been referred by David and that Michael was someone he might be interested in. David's name, of course, was the ultimate door-opener in the music business, and Bruce agreed to meet with us in Los Angeles.

During a short break from the tour, we took a Bublé family trip down to L.A. in February—Amber, Michael, Michael's sister Crystal and I—and stayed with their family friend, a gracious woman everyone called Aunt Grace.

Michael and I met Bruce at his home studio. He was so very charming, ever the gentleman. Michael sang a few songs that Bruce taped. He thought Michael was really talented and said he wanted to try to sell *BaBalu* on the

This photo was taken in 2001 when we went to LA to meet with agent Bruce Roberts, who had worked with such talents as Cher, Barbra Streisand and Celine Dion.

Home Shopping Network. He tried for a time afterward, but it never worked out.

We enjoyed our time with him in L.A. and went back home so that Michael could rejoin the tour. I would see Bruce at various events while in Los Angeles, and he always had such kind things to say about Michael and was so supportive of me and my work with Michael. We still correspond from time to time.

When *Forever Swing* ended—the last show was in Montreal on April 1—Michael and Debbie moved back to Vancouver, into the same apartment complex I was living in, and he started a series of appearances at various venues and events, including an Amway convention in Maui.

He and his old band were also hired to play at an exclusive club in Cape Canaveral in mid-April, courtesy of Brian Mulroney, who had told many of his friends about Michael and encouraged them to book him at their various fundraising and private events. He also referred us to a good immigration lawyer, who helped us sort out some of the working visa issues we were increasingly running into with Michael going back and forth to work across the Canada-U.S. border.

Michael liked these jobs, but it was still the same old story. He felt he wasn't getting anywhere and would always ask me: "What's going to happen, Bev?"

I could understand his frustration, but to me it was a process. "Think of it as connect the dots," I would tell him. "People see you, they tell other people and when the day comes—not *if* the day comes—they're going to remember that they saw you, and I believe that will be good for your career."

"Okay, Bevy," he would say.

One day, Andrew Van Slee, a Canadian-born film director, phoned me out of the blue and said he was shooting a movie in L.A. called *Totally Blonde*, which was about a young woman who dyes her hair blonde and goes in search of Mr. Right. They had another singer they were hiring to be in the movie, but that person had bowed out, so they wanted Michael to play the crooner character named Van Martin. It was short notice. He had to be on the set June 12.

I thought it would be good for Michael, and he did, too. He wanted to check into it a bit, and wondered what his role would be and what he would be singing, but he was excited about not just singing but also acting in a movie.

That May, I had a lovely diversion from all the chaos when Daniel, who was flying small planes around the Pacific Northwest, asked me to join him for a Mother's Day date that had become a tradition for the pilots of the small Washington State airline he was working for. He picked me up in Vancouver and we flew over to Victoria, where we joined all the other pilots and their mothers at the famed Empress Hotel for afternoon tea. I wasn't wild about the little plane, or flying low over the water across the channel, but it was the first time I had ever flown with him when he was the pilot, and it was one of the most special days of my life.

Meanwhile, Andrew had sent me a contract. I was worried about making sure that Michael only sang in the movie and nothing, like a soundtrack with him on it, would be done afterward. He assured me that was the case, we exchanged signatures and I booked Michael's flight. We had a week to get him to Hollywood.

A few days after Michael settled in Hollywood, I went down to visit him. He was living with Richard Naegele, one of the producers of *Totally Blonde* and a truly generous man, who opened his home to Michael and Debbie, not only giving them a place to live but making them feel very welcome. His house on Angelo Drive had a good vibe. It had once belonged to Frank Sinatra Jr., which seemed fitting, and had also been home to musical legends such as Stevie Nicks, and Jennifer Lopez and P. Diddy.

Nathan Folks, also a producer on the movie, took Michael under his wing, and they became good friends. They had parties at the house and would go out on the town, which was Nathan's way of introducing Michael to the L.A. social scene. Once, when Nathan picked up his father from the airport, he took Michael along and Michael serenaded Nathan's dad with a song he had just written, prompting yet another comparison to Sinatra from a delighted Folks Sr.

Nathan knew that *Totally Blonde* wasn't exactly *Citizen Kane*, that the script was weak, but he kept reassuring Michael that his singing was the highlight, that his fame would eventually far outshine the movie, should it be a flop, which ultimately it was.

Nathan was equally gracious when dealing with me, but he and the others working on the movie weren't sure I was going to be able to get Michael where he needed to go. Part of the problem, Nathan said, was that I was in Vancouver, a million miles away from the centre of the entertainment universe.

Mercifully, *Totally Blonde* was a short shoot, but while Michael and Debbie were still in L.A., I decided it was time I talked directly to David. I had only dealt with him indirectly and had never even talked to him on the phone, even though it had been almost a year since he met Michael at the Mulroney wedding and began booking him for events.

So I picked up the phone, called David's number, got his secretary and asked her if I could speak to David. He came on the line, and after a few pleasantries, I said: "David, are you ever going to work with Michael?"

I went into my usual Michael sales pitch: "David, he's so talented; I know this will work, with all my heart."

I must have caught him off guard. He stammered: "Well, uh, er," and then said: "You know what? We need to have a three-way conversation, you, me and Michael."

David said he would arrange for his assistant to get the three of us together on a conference call. A few days later, he did.

When Michael, David and I were on the phone, I started bragging about Michael, but David kept getting interrupted by other more important phone calls. Once, when he put us on hold, I said to Michael: "Oh, my God, Michael, I can't believe we're talking to David Foster," and Michael said, "Bev, Bev, calm down. You know what? He probably has us on mute now and he's listening to us and listening to you acting like this crazy woman. Bev, you've gotta calm down."

There was no calming me down. "Michael, you know what? I don't care if he's listening, because he will love the fact that I'm so excited, and Michael, I don't care, I'm so excited that we're talking to him and that he's giving us the time of day."

David kept coming back and forth on the line. Finally, he said to me: "Okay, Beverly. Here's the thing. If you can raise $450,000 in US funds, I will produce a CD for Michael." Without hesitation, I said: "David, I will get the money."

With that, he said "keep in touch" and hung up the phone. Michael was apoplectic: "Bev, are you crazy?! Where are you going to get that kind of money!?"

I was unfazed. "Michael, if David Foster is going to produce your CD, I will find that money. That's our calling card, Michael."

Back home, I started beating the bushes, phoning some of the biggest fundraisers in the Vancouver area. One name that came up was Nash Jiwa. I met with him, told him the whole Michael–David Foster story and gave him a copy of *BaBalu*. He told me he was impressed with the CD and my "love for this young man" and would see what he could do, but there were no guarantees.

A week later, Nash phoned me. He'd had no luck, he said, even though he had called many of his deep-pocket contacts looking for an investor to underwrite a David Foster–produced CD for Michael. The problem, he said, was that "nobody believes that it costs $450,000 to make a CD. Nobody. I'm sorry, I can't help you."

I thanked him for trying, and that was the end of that. I knew it was a lot of money, but it was David Foster, after all, one of the most successful and revered music producers in the business, and I knew that music videos alone at the time, one featuring Michael Jackson, for instance, were costing millions. Meanwhile, Michael was back in Vancouver, singing occasionally at Carnegie's restaurant over the summer but still on call for David, who had him flying off now and then to perform at various events. I knew this was David's way of testing the waters with new talent, and it was brilliant: virtually risk-free for him and great exposure for Michael.

At one of his Carnegie shows that summer of 2001, local DJ Jack Cullen, renowned for his late-night Owl Prowl radio show and his huge private record collection, was in the audience. He had been a supporter of Michael's from early on and had him on his show frequently. On this night, Michael sang a few up-tempo songs, and when he was done, he walked over to Jack and said: "How did I do, Jack?" Jack looked at him and said: "Sing a ballad, Michael." And so he did, serenading the room with "I'll Never Smile Again," a song, legend had it, that made the owlish Jack smile.

In mid-August, with no CD money in sight, I called David to chat about my concerns, and he said it might be a good idea for me to meet Los Angeles agent Barry Krost. I had been researching management companies, still looking for the right person to help us, so I called Barry, dropped the magic name of Foster, and Michael and I were once again heading back to Los Angeles.

We met with Barry at his office. Such a colourful guy, always smiling, a great personality. I really liked him and thought it would be fun to work with him.

He took us to lunch at Mr. Chow, a Beverly Hills hot spot known for its exquisite Asian cuisine, and we talked. Barry liked Michael, loved his voice, and I told him our story, that we were trying to raise money and needed a good agent to steer us in the right direction. We discussed what he might do for Michael, but there were so many famous people coming and going that I couldn't help gawking. Barry would point out certain people, and Michael, as always, would tell me not to stare.

We finished lunch and promised to stay in touch. We did for a time, but like so many others we had approached for advice and help, Barry couldn't seem to take it anywhere. He loved Michael, and his talent, but, again, didn't really know what to do with him.

Not too long after, Michael played at a private party at David's house in Malibu, co-hosted with his wife, Linda Thompson, and David invited me to join them. It seemed like everyone in Hollywood was at that party—Tony Danza, Kelsey Grammer, Brooke Shields, Ed McMahon, Kenny G and so many others—but I was thrilled because I was finally going to meet David in person.

Ever the consummate host, he sent a car to pick us up at our hotel just before the event so that we could chat in private for a bit, and Michael said: "Wait 'til you meet him, Bev. His hair is always kerfuffled, his socks will be rolled down, he looks like he just got out of bed and he always smells spicy."

The car drove up to the big double gates, got buzzed in and when the gates swung open, I couldn't believe how grand it was. The grounds were as big as Stanley Park, with tennis courts and a swimming pool and even a little tram to take people from the bottom of the sloping lawn up to the house. It was beautiful.

We went into the house and, sure enough, there was David, coming down the stairs exactly as Michael had described him: khaki-coloured shorts, navy blue sweatshirt, white socks rolled down and his hair all kerfuffled.

I kissed and hugged him, and he smelled spicy. I liked him right away.

We sat in the living room and talked about *BaBalu* and Michael's chances in the industry. David said it was difficult, that Harry Connick Jr. had cornered the crooner market and there wasn't much room for another singer of that type. Michael told him of his frustration, how nothing was happening for him and how we couldn't seem to get that break we needed.

It was something I had heard from Michael so many times before, and I understood his impatience, and I said: "David, I can never convince Michael that it's happening the way it's supposed to happen. Because he thinks it should be yesterday, and I don't feel it has to be yesterday, because of the way the industry is."

David nodded: "Michael, you've got a helluva voice, but it's scary because of the genre."

And then it was time for the party, a magnificent banquet and entertainment that included a performance by Kenny G. Michael also sang a few songs, his regulars like "All of Me," and when it was over and everyone started leaving, I spotted Kelsey Grammer. I have seen every *Frasier* episode and couldn't believe I was in the same room with one of my favourite television actors.

Michael knew how I felt about Kelsey Grammer, looked at me and said, teasing me like he always did: "Bev, don't you dare walk up to anyone."

"Michael, I promise I won't," I said. And then when he wasn't looking, I walked over to Kelsey, who was helping his wife, Camille, into her coat. I said, "Kelsey, I'm not supposed to do this, but I'm Michael Bublé's manager, and I love you and I love your show. I've seen every episode over and over."

Kelsey looked at me and, with the biggest grin you can imagine, said: "You can never hear that too much."

One of the people David introduced us to at the party was Brian Avnet, Josh Groban's manager. He, too, loved Michael, thought he was talented and said he would love to represent him but wasn't sure how that would work, but he would be happy to talk about it sometime. Brian assured me, too, that if we ever teamed up, he would honour my relationship with Michael, that he respected the work I had done. It was, despite all that I had heard about the backstabbing nature of the industry, something I would hear over and over again, from agents and managers and would-be investors, and even from David, and I was so grateful for that.

These were people I knew I could trust.

In Vancouver, in late August, Michael was back headlining the Pacific National Exhibition, where he had been "discovered" six years before, and it wasn't lost on either one of us how odd it seemed that one weekend he would be singing for David Foster and hobnobbing with the Hollywood elite and the next be on stage playing his hometown agricultural fair.

It was a perfect, and frustrating, example of what was working for us and what, in many ways, wasn't.

And then came September 11, 2001, and everyone's world changed.

Shortly after the terrorist attacks that felled Manhattan's Twin Towers and killed thousands, David called Michael and said that because no one was flying out of fear of future attacks, comedian and *Tonight Show* host Jay Leno had decided to hold two free concerts in Las Vegas on the weekend of September 29. A frequent headliner in Vegas, he had heard that tourism had been flagging since 9/11. The shows would be at the 1,700-seat EFX Theater in the MGM Grand, and Jay asked only that ticket holders tip their servers well.

David was a friend of Leno's, and when he heard about the comedian's plans, he made arrangements for Michael to open the shows. He wouldn't be paid, of course, but we were over the moon.

Amber and the whole family drove Michael and me to the airport. We were so excited, and as the plane headed south toward Las Vegas, I never felt safer, or surer this might be Michael's moment. Something told me that this might be the break. We still didn't have the $450,000, but I just had a feeling that this was it. The big break.

It was a great show. Michael sang and got a wonderful response from the audience, including a huge ovation as he was leaving the stage, except he realized later that most of it was for Leno, who was coming out onstage as Michael was heading into the wings. Michael laughed about it afterward, and we watched Leno's show and it was terrific. Such a funny man. Jay was also very complimentary of

Michael, and as the evening wound down, we were feeling good about things.

The next morning, a Sunday, David phoned Michael in his room and said: "You and Bev need to get in a cab and get over here to the Mirage. I'm here with Paul Anka. He's a friend of mine, and I think he can help us."

Paul Anka. Ottawa-born singer and songwriter, teenage idol, the 1950s crooner who sold millions of records with hits including "Diana" and "Put Your Head on My Shoulder," the man who wrote songs such as "My Way," for Frank Sinatra, and "She's a Lady," for Tom Jones. A music legend.

I said: "Oh my God, Michael, he's my idol."

We got to the Mirage, walked down a long hallway and knocked on the door of Paul's room.

David and Linda and Paul and his lady friend were all in luxurious white robes, seated at a big table, having brunch. David introduced us to Paul and I told him how excited I was to meet him. Paul looked at me and said: "Okay, tell me the story."

We sat at the table and had coffee, and I told Paul everything, about Michael's start and the *BaBalu* CD and all the people we had asked for help who never came through for us and how we couldn't raise the $450,000 that David needed for the new CD.

I knew Paul liked me because of my sincerity, because when I talked about Michael, it was always from the heart, because that's just the way I felt. I told him we needed help and that I didn't even know what that looked like, but that all this time we had just been looking for someone to find us. I think that touched him.

When David wandered off to use the telephone, Paul turned to me and said: "I think I can help you. I think I can get the money for David to produce the CD."

Well, of course, I cried.

David got off the phone and looked over and said: "Why is Bev crying?"

"Well, she's verklempt," said Michael, "because Paul said he could help us."

David looked at Paul, and we knew that they had already talked about it.

Linda and Paul's lady friend decided to go for a massage, so Paul and David and Michael and I went out onto the patio and talked some more. And then Paul asked Michael to sing for him.

David arranged for us to use a room in the Mirage that had a piano. When Paul and David went off to get changed, Michael, who had always given me such a hard time for wearing my heart on my sleeve, said: "Bev, that was really good. You've got to learn to cry on demand."

The four of us walked down the hall and into a room with a black baby grand. David sat down at the piano, Michael stood near him and Paul sat down on a chair beside me, arms crossed, sunglasses on, his head down and covered by a baseball cap. Michael, with David accompanying him, launched into several songs, including "My Way." When he was done, the room was quiet. Paul looked up and said, softly: "Yeah, yeah, it's good. It's good."

Nobody said much after that, and then we got up to leave. When we got to the door, I hugged Paul and said how great it had been to meet him, and he said to me, just like that: "I can help you."

"Really?"

"Really."

And then he said he would call me on Tuesday.

And, of course, I cried.

Michael and I hopped into a cab and went back to the hotel to pack, because we had a flight to catch. We called his family and told them what had just happened and everyone was on cloud nine. Michael was beyond excited but still apprehensive: Did Paul really think he was talented? "Do you really think this will happen, Bev?" He said it over and over. The truth is we were both a little shell-shocked, because this was Paul Anka, and Paul Anka was telling us he could help us.

On Monday, back home in Vancouver, I called everyone I knew and told them that we had met Paul Anka and that, finally, after all these years of being lost, we might have been found.

I was at home on Tuesday when, at 2 p.m., the phone rang.

"Beverly, this is Paul Anka."

I paused. "Paul, is it really you? Because Paul, listen, I called everybody I know to tell them I met you, and my friends and I always play tricks on each other and I don't know your voice well enough. Is it really you?"

"Bev," he said. "I have $450,000 for David to make Michael's CD. So do you think this is me?"

And, of course, I cried.

And then I said: "Well, what do we do now?"

And Paul Anka said: "You and Michael need to come to L.A."

CHAPTER SIX

A Year in Los Angeles

When Paul Anka tells you that he has $450,000 to make your CD, and David Foster says he will produce the CD, and when those two music industry titans tell you that you need to come to Los Angeles, as soon as possible, because they want to start recording that CD, you can't get on a plane fast enough.

But Michael had something he needed to do first.

He wanted to make another CD, a personal one, dedicated to Mitch. It was his grandfather, after all, who had introduced him to the music he would come to love, the music that would define his career. Michael decided to produce the CD himself, and it was engineered in Gabriel Hasselbach's home studio for Silver Lining Management. Gabriel played trumpet, flute, digital winds, strings and the accordion while Ron Thompson played guitar.

Dream had thirteen songs, all favourites of grandfather and grandson: "Dream," "Anema E Core," "I'll Never Smile Again," "Stardust," "You Always Hurt the One You

In 2001, Michael recorded a special dedication CD to his two grandfathers. Grandfather Frank Bublé had recently passed away and grandfather Mitch Santaga introduced him to the music he grew to love. He performed a tribute concert at the Vogue Theatre, and the money raised from the CD sales was given to cancer research.

Love," "Don't Be a Baby, Baby," "Maria Elena," "Daddy's Little Girl," "Paper Doll," "Surrender," "Till Then," "You Belong to Me" and "I Wish You Love."

Only one hundred copies were pressed, and they were sold at a special concert Michael arranged at the Vogue Theatre on November 11, 2001. Inside the CD was Michael's dedication:

This was supposed to be a single recording as a birthday gift for my grandpa Santaga. You see, the reason that I fell in love with the music of this era was because of him playing it for me as long as I could remember. For his birthday, I decided I would go into the studio and record some of his very favourite songs for his personal use only—not to be released, not to be copied.

Well, that changed a short time later when our family found out my other grandpa Bublé had been diagnosed with cancer. It didn't take very long for me to decide that I wanted to help in some way, and this was my way. I would put out a limited number of this CD and give proceeds to cancer research. This record did not cost a million dollars to make, does not have a huge symphony and does not have elaborate production. What it does have is every ounce of love that I have for my family and friends and this incredible music. I hope it will be a lasting legacy for two of the greatest men that I will ever know.

Enjoy!
Michael

It was the perfect gift.

It was also time to start thinking about the move. Michael and I had packed up once before, moving to Toronto from Vancouver in 2000, in what would be a somewhat lacklustre effort to advance his career, but we both knew, intuitively, that his future was in L.A., so we started making plans.

He and I flew down in January of 2002, once again staying with Aunt Grace, to look for a place to live. Everything was expensive—even the dumps were $2,000 a month—but Nathan Folks, whom Michael and Debbie had stayed with during the *Totally Blonde* shoot, was kind enough to take us around to look at apartments.

Naturally, we found time to visit with David and Paul

Michael and me on the airplane in March 2002, heading off to Los Angeles to live.

while we were there—Paul took us to dinner a lot, usually at the Ivy, a celebrity favourite—but we didn't forget for one minute that our immediate goal was to find a place to live.

Of all the apartments Nathan showed us, the one we liked the most was in Westwood, near UCLA, in a brand new walk-up with air conditioning. It was posh. The lobby was decorated beautifully, always with fresh flowers. There was a twenty-four-hour concierge and a pool out back ringed by stainless steel barbecues and trendy patio furniture. The apartment was roomy. It had two bedrooms and two bathrooms, and nice living and dining rooms. Michael took the master bedroom, with the big sunken tub, and I took the other bed and bath on the opposite side of the suite. The apartment didn't have a view, because we were at the back of the building, but there was a deck, lovely gardens and a workout facility.

It was a great location but pricey at $3,900 rent a month. We signed a year-long lease, effective March 1, 2002.

When we got back to Vancouver, I called Paul and told him that we had found a place, that I had given notice in Vancouver and had booked movers.

"Now Paul," I said, "you know that we gave our notices here and we're moving to L.A., right?" He said, "Yes," like it was no big deal. To him, the move was obvious and necessary. For us, there was excitement, but

The Westwood building in Los Angeles where Michael and I shared an apartment from 2002 to 2003, while Michael recorded his self-titled CD with David Foster.

there was also nervousness about what might lie ahead, because once again, we just didn't know.

My friends and family, though, were actually starting to believe that this was turning into something real and didn't even blink when I told them I was moving to California with Michael. It was as if they expected nothing less.

It's not that I had doubts, but I wasn't really sure why I was doing it, except that I was so invested in Michael that it seemed like a natural thing to do. The truth is that no other manager would move with their client to another city, much less live with that client, but I wasn't like other managers. Michael was my only client, and it was as if he was my own son. I just did it. I knew I had to, because who else would? And nobody, not my family or friends, or Michael's family, ever seemed to question it.

For Michael, as big as this move was, as thrilling as the prospects were, he still carried a sense of uncertainty about his future.

If he understood that this chase for stardom could be an excruciating and frustrating process, he never admitted it to me. He conceded, however, in an interview published earlier in *The Vancouver Sun*, that, as I had been telling him, success was partly about being in the right place at the right time. "Well, consistently, I have been in the right place at the right time," he told the writer. "And it's funny, because the whole time it seemed to me that I was in the wrong place at the wrong time."

And we had been at this for seven years, hardscrabbling our way along this long road to what we hoped was success. Michael's holy grail had always been to sign a record deal, and in his mind, that meant signing a contract with one of the big names in the music industry: Sony or Warner Bros. And now, because David was connected to Warner Bros. (he was an executive, in fact), all Michael's hopes were channelled toward a deal with Warner.

This is why we both knew that if anything was going to happen, it would happen in Los Angeles in 2002.

I put some of my things in storage but decided to ship my furniture, including my bed, filing cabinet and all my dishes and pots and pans, down to the new L.A. apartment. Debbie and Michael gave up their place, too, and Debbie stored most of her things at her parents' home in Tsawwassen while Michael moved some of his stuff to his parents' house in Burnaby. Together they didn't really have much to take, beyond their personal belongings, so we pooled all our things on one truck and sent them south.

Debbie stayed behind in Vancouver to wrap up a few loose ends, and Michael and I flew to Los Angeles on March 6, 2002.

We had barely lifted off from the Vancouver tarmac when Michael turned to me and said: "You know, you don't even really have to be going down here. Your work is done; you've worked your ass off all these years. I'll tell you what. When I get my money, I'll pay you $100,000 for every year you were with me, and then you can go home and eat popcorn."

He said it, I know, because he probably wanted to live on his own in L.A., and who could blame him? Here he was, a charming twenty-six-year-old talent on the verge of what we hoped was stardom, embarking on an exciting new adventure—perhaps the biggest of his life—and here

I was, a sixty-two-year-old soon-to-be grandmother, not only tagging along but moving in with him.

But Michael, being Michael, was too respectful, and he couldn't just come right out and ask me not to come.

And the truth is that he needed me, and I think, deep down, he knew that.

"Michael," I told him, "my work is not done. We are only moving to L.A. We still don't know what's going to happen. Tell me what you think is going to happen? Are we signed with anyone? Do we have a manager? What's going to happen, Michael?" And that was the end of the conversation.

Our furniture arrived at the same time we did, but when we got there the first thing we did was call David, who told us, in no uncertain terms, that we needed to get cell phones, and by that he meant Verizon phones, the kind that worked in the U.S., unlike our Canadian mobiles. Communication was all important.

A few days after we arrived, on March 11, we received a formal invitation to attend a reception and banquet hosted by the Canadian consul general in Los Angeles, Colin Robertson, who was honouring Paul Anka's forty-fourth anniversary in show business. The event was held at the consul residence in Hancock Park and was jam-packed with celebrities and dignitaries. David was there, of course, with Linda, along with Wayne Gretzky and his wife, Janet Jones-Gretzky, Larry and Shawn King, Robert and Linell Shapiro, Jeff and Deborah Wald, Burt and Jane Bacharach and so many others.

David introduced us to everyone: "This is Michael and his manager, Beverly," he would say. At one point, I was standing with Michael when Robert Shapiro came over and said, "Michael Bublé, I'm Robert Shapiro. I'm glad to meet you. I understand you're with David Foster."

Michael turned to me and said, "This is my manager, Beverly," and before you could say "foot in mouth," I blurted out: "Oh, Mr. Shapiro, I know who you are, from Vancouver."

Robert looked puzzled but shook our hands and said he was looking forward to hearing more about Michael down the road, and walked away.

Michael was disgusted, and he never really got mad at me, but this time he was not happy. "Bev, you don't know him from Temple Sholom. He's O.J. Simpson's lawyer."

I had confused Robert Shapiro with Murray Shapiro, a Vancouver lawyer. I wanted to die right there. Michael walked away from me. I was mortified. A few minutes later, before we sat down for dinner, I saw that Robert was alone and went over to him and said: "Mr. Shapiro, I want to die." He said, "Why is that, dear?" and I told him that I was embarrassed that I had mixed him up with another lawyer I knew back home. He was lovely about it, and said it happened all the time, that people were always thinking he was someone else, simply because they recognized him from being on television during the Simpson trial.

"You know what?" he said. "I have been to Vancouver, and Vancouver's a beautiful city."

The rest of the evening was wonderful. Michael was at his most charming and having a great time, and everyone thought he was adorable.

We had only been in Los Angeles for a short time when Paul presented Michael and me with a contract,

tied to the $450,000 investment. It was thick and compli-
cated, and it would have tied us up for some time, and I
knew that could mean a record label wouldn't touch us.
David confirmed that it would be an issue for a future
signing opportunity, so even though Michael wasn't
with a label at that moment, we had to tell Paul that we
couldn't sign it.

I felt terrible, we both did, but I had always been so
careful about shackling Michael to any contract, even if it
was with Paul Anka, even if it meant not getting the money
to produce the CD. So I told Paul that I wasn't comfortable
with it, and he understood, but I know he was disappointed, because we all knew that he had really been the
only one who had stepped up to the plate to help Michael.
He would, of course, still be involved with the CD, which
is what we all wanted. And Michael, to show his gratitude
and respect, subsequently made a verbal contract with him
that saw Paul get a percentage from the sales of the CD.

Although we were living what we thought was the
high life in L.A., we didn't have much money. Before we
had left Vancouver, Michael's grandparents had given him
$30,000 to keep us going. They had been his benefactors
from day one, and he, as always, vowed to pay them back,
but Yolanda would always tell her grandson not to worry
because, "You're going to have it anyway when we die."

And David, knowing our situation, was also unbe-
lievably generous, which we were learning was just his
way, giving us $20,000 to help pay for incidentals while
we were there. Michael also made a bit of money from
some of the performances David arranged, and Nathan
was kind enough to loan Michael a car, his old Chrysler

convertible, to help us get around town. Debbie, who was still pursuing her own career in Vancouver, was back and forth between the two cities, but when she was in L.A., the three of us went everywhere in that car.

David was keen to start working on the CD, and it wasn't long after our arrival before Michael and I found ourselves at Paul's house for a brainstorming session. His place was a beautiful gated mansion, a huge home and so cozy, and he was the ultimate host. The house was up in the hills on Mulholland Drive and had a gorgeous view, and when we arrived, Paul's housekeeper had set the table with a wonderful spread so that we wouldn't go hungry.

We convened in the music room, which had a piano, and started talking about what songs might go on the CD. We knew they'd all be covers from the American song-book, not originals, so we talked about all the crooner songs that would best suit Michael's voice. Michael didn't want too much Sinatra on the CD, because, as always, he was worried that he'd sing himself into a corner as a Sinatra clone. He loved Sinatra, and liked being compared to him, but he always insisted he wasn't the next Sinatra.

It was hard to pick the songs, because there were just so many, like "Mack the Knife," which was one of Michael's favourites but ironically didn't make the cut. Paul and David always asked my opinion, and I was pleased that they did. I would think to myself, here I am in Paul Anka's home, with David Foster and Michael Bublé, and they're asking me my opinion about what songs Michael should sing on his first big CD. Who gets to do that? I'd say to myself. Why, Beverly Delich, from Butte, Montana, that's who.

After a time, the list was whittled down to the thirteen songs that were eventually recorded on the Michael Bublé CD. It was an eclectic mix of vintage and modern that included "Fever," "Summer Wind," "Moondance," "Crazy Little Thing Called Love," "For Once in My Life" and "Put Your Head on My Shoulder," which was written by Paul and had been a huge hit for him in 1959.

As we began preparing to go into the studio and start recording, I was still looking for someone to help co-manage Michael with me. Paul was travelling a lot, but I sought his advice all the time. Once, while I was eating in a shopping mall, I called Paul and told him that I wasn't making any headway with Josh Groban's manager, Brian Avnet, whom I had spoken to about Michael at David's urging.

I still wanted to work with someone, someone who knew more than I did, who could help me move Michael along, and who could teach me a lot more about the business. I just wanted to learn and needed someone who wouldn't be threatened by me. I was willing to do anything that needed to be done, no matter how menial, but wasn't having any luck finding that right co-manager. But Brian was tied up with Josh, who was being produced by David, and one day he said he couldn't do it, because Josh was too big of a commitment for him. I was disappointed, but I understood.

And David told me that Paul was too busy doing his own thing, which still included performing, to help me find a co-manager, so I was on my own.

Before long, Michael and I fell into a routine, heading every day to David's studio to work on the CD. It was a bit of a drive, and we'd pile into Nathan's car (and stop at McDonald's on the way), but it wasn't long before David began sending a Town Car to pick us up. We'd usually leave mid-morning, to avoid the infamous Los Angeles traffic jams.

David's studio was separate from his house and was very large. There was an office for his assistant, a kitchen, a big soundboard, surrounded by every music award you can imagine, and, in another nearby room, the actual recording studio. I would sit on the couch, David would sit at the soundboard or the piano and we would watch Michael on a TV monitor, crooning into the mike in an adjacent room.

In the studio would be me, David, Michael, David's assistant and sometimes Debbie, and I would make coffee, but every once in a while, David would give me his credit card and I'd head out for a Starbucks latte run down the hill from the house. And, again, it would occur to me: Who gets to go shopping with David Foster's American Express platinum card? Why, Beverly Delich, of Butte, Montana, that's who, I'd say right back.

David had a decent enough coffee pot, but Paul, who came into the studio whenever he could, decided we needed a deluxe $3,000 coffee machine and had one installed in the studio. None of us could figure out how to work it. One day, Paul came in and when we confessed that we hadn't used his gift, he laughed and said: "What the hell is wrong with you guys?" David said: "I've tried.

Bev has tried." So Paul taught us to use the machine, but truth be told, David still liked his Starbucks.

Every day, Michael would go into the recording booth and sing the song they had selected that day. David would then analyze the result and decide what changes would be made. If they disagreed, which they did on occasion, David would respect Michael's insistence that the work had to represent him, and they would work on it until they came up with the combination of music and lyrics they could both live with.

We did a lot of eating during those sessions, and David and Linda were wonderful hosts. Some days, we'd go up to the house and Linda would have her staff cook us lunch. Once, they invited us to join them for a dinner out and took us to an Asian restaurant, because Michael and Linda love sushi. It was an amazing place, and pricey. David, sitting beside me, said: "Bev, do you like this shit? I hate this shit." I confessed that I wasn't crazy about sushi, and he said, "Do you like steak?" When I said yes, he ordered us steak.

Sometimes, during a recording session, we'd break for lunch and either head out to a wonderful Greek restaurant that David liked or order in plates of pita and hummus and delicious chicken dishes from the same place. And the studio was stocked with a bottomless supply of candy and other goodies, stashed in cupboards and on shelves all over the place. Pringles. Red licorice. Jelly beans. It came as no surprise that, after a few months, we started getting a little chubby.

As a rule, we'd work from noonish until about eleven at night, every day except Sunday. Often, in the middle

Michael, Paul Anka and David Foster in 2002, working in David's home studio in Malibu.

Legendary Chilean producer Humberto Gatica (front) works on the album with Michael, David Foster and Paul Anka at Warner Bros. Studio. Gatica also worked with artists such as Michael Jackson, Barbra Streisand, Madonna and Mariah Carey.

of an intensive recording session, the boys would need a break, so Michael and David and Humberto Gatica, a producer and sound mixer who was also working on the CD, would play tennis on the courts that were on the grounds, while I went for a walk or on a little shopping trip at the strip mall down the hill.

Michael told me later that, during one of those tennis breaks, David asked him: "So, how is Bev doing?" I think they both thought I was bored. I was anything but, and I told him so. I loved it, never missed a session and learned so much. I had waited so long for it.

After the songs for the CD were selected, David would line up the musicians and the backup vocals to come in and record the layers of music that would make up each track. Michael would then come back in and sing over the finished music, to ensure the timing was spot on. Every musician had to make several takes of every song, and Michael had to record every song sometimes up to ten times, but he was enthralled with the whole process, and it was as if he had been born to the recording studio. He was intense and completely committed to doing his best, and going to the studio every day became his new way of life.

Here he was, Michael Bublé, the Burnaby boy from the PNE, recording a CD with David Foster, and if, on the surface, it couldn't get any better than that, I knew he was still uneasy that we hadn't found a co-manager. And there was no contract with a record company, either. Even David's pull at Warner Bros. had gotten us nowhere. The label, he told us, was skeptical about signing Michael.

That uneasiness wasn't helped by a phone call I got one day from David.

"You know, Bev," he said, "this could all turn to shit, and you'll have to go home."

What he meant was that nothing might come of the CD, which he was underwriting without asking for anything from us (he had his own label, 143 Records), and we "would just chalk it up. I would never expect that you would pay. I would just absorb it."

But we all soldiered on, knowing that no matter the outcome, we were where we needed to be.

I loved all the songs on the CD, because I loved everything Michael sang, but "How Can You Mend a Broken Heart" and "Kissing a Fool" were my favourites. Michael did such a beautiful job on them. And even after all his protests, he ended up singing two Sinatra classics—"Summer Wind" and "Come Fly with Me"— because David finally convinced him that he had to, telling him: "You know, Michael, let's face it. You are that genre, so we have to put something Sinatra on there."

David had contacted two renowned composers to contribute to the arrangements on the CD: Bill Holman and Johnny Mandel, two industry greats.

Bill, whose musical resumé included being hired by Stan Kenton to play the saxophone and doing arrangements for greats from Woody Herman and Count Basie to Buddy Rich and Ella Fitzgerald, came in and worked on "Fever." He was a quiet, gracious man and even had us over to his home.

Juilliard-trained Johnny Mandel, who had worked with everyone from Sinatra to Peggy Lee, came in and wrote the score and produced "That's All." One morning, when we were in the recording studio, David said he had to go out for an appointment and that Johnny would be coming by about eleven. He told us Johnny had a certain way of working.

"This is exactly what he's like," David said. "He'll come in, kick off his shoes, go over to the piano, sit down and he'll say to you something like 'this is a little like what it should go like, right?' And he'll play a little of the tune and Michael will say 'yeah,' and then he'll chat a little bit, a little about the weather, nothing big, nothing technical, and then he'll put on his shoes and he'll leave."

Johnny arrived at eleven, and that's exactly what happened. Right down to the shoes. David came back and said: "Well, was it exactly like I told you?"

We said yes, and that it was perfect.

Based on that visit to the studio, Johnny wrote individual charts for a twenty-plus-piece orchestra. Each musician, hired on a union contract, was advised by David to arrive on time at the Warner Bros. studio, where "That's All" was being recorded, and precisely at 10 a.m., Johnny came in, tapped his baton, and they played the song.

Michael, David and I were watching and listening from another room—we were separated from the orchestra by a glass wall—and when they started playing, we got goosebumps. David, who was sitting at a soundboard, turned to us and said: "Fuck, huh. Fuck." Then it was Michael's turn. He went in and sang live with the orchestra.

When they were done, David decided he wanted a few notes changed. He was worried about asking Johnny, because he considered him the master of the craft, but decided to give it a whirl. Johnny came out of the studio, and David said: "Fuck, man, fuck, it just blew our minds.

Now there's just something I wanted to ask you, just a teeny tiny thing. Would you mind..."

And Johnny Mandel listened to what he had to say, and then said to David Foster: "What for?"

Recording the CD wasn't Michael's only job during those months. People were well aware of David's philanthropic nature and were always asking him to appear and help raise money for their particular charities. David often obliged, and he and Michael performed all over, in Santa Barbara and Phoenix, at the Beverly Hilton Hotel and with Kenny G.

Once, Michael and I were invited to Ed McMahon's house for a function. Like Paul, he lived up on Mulholland Drive. Michael was driving. We had leased a car at this point, but even though it was the same route we'd take to Paul's house, we got lost. We always got lost, and Michael always blamed me, even though we usually had maps or had looked it up. It was crazy, because I was always sure we knew where we were going.

While we were driving, Lisa called me.

"Lisa, I can't talk. We're on our way to Ed McMahon's house, we're lost, we're running out of gas and we're late."

As I was hanging up, I heard her turn to her work-mates and say, "Okay, here's what's happening today with my mother..."

We pulled over and called Paul. He said, very calmly as usual: "Come to my house and we'll go from here." He and David, who was at Paul's house, were going to Ed's function as well.

We got to Paul's house and found the two of them

sitting at the table, eating and having a great time. David looked up at us—I guess we were quite a sight—shook his head and said: "Jesus Christ, you two." We joined them for a little snack and then Paul drove us to Ed McMahon's party in his car.

Another event was in Palm Springs, at the Indian Wells Tennis Garden. Michael and I had taken a Town Car and stayed at a gorgeous country club. We each had a lovely room, with outdoor patios and Spanish tiles in the bathrooms. It was a quick trip, though, just overnight, and we had to get into rehearsal as soon as we arrived. But right after we checked in, Michael was informed that David had arranged for him to play tennis in a doubles match against Wayne Newton. Michael never played tennis that seriously, which was a good thing, because when they were introduced before the match, Wayne said to him jokingly, "Michael Bublé, if you win, you will never perform in Las Vegas." I immediately called Lisa and said, "Oh, my God, Lisa. You can't believe it. Michael is playing tennis with Wayne Newton!"

Michael and his tennis partner lost the match.

During those months, Michael also performed at a private function for industrialist Marvin Davis and his socialite wife, Barbara, at their Los Angeles home, which was filled to overflowing with A-list movie stars such as Barbra Streisand, Elizabeth Taylor and Tom Hanks. As Michael and I went into the green room, I was thrilled to run into Tom and shook hands with him. After Michael performed, Elizabeth Taylor told him she was smitten and loved his voice. For Michael, it was a huge compliment, to be recognized for his talent by such an entertainment industry icon.

In May, Michael, Debbie and I flew to Las Vegas, at Paul's invitation. He had a bronze-coloured limousine waiting for us at the airport, which took us to the Mirage. Paul had reserved a luxurious suite for us, with chandeliers, a living room and a full-service kitchen with a separate dining room. There was even a beautiful gift box filled with cheeses and crackers, nuts and candy and wine. Michael and Debbie's room had a bed on a raised platform with a remote-controlled television that rose up at the foot of the bed.

One of Paul's assistants was there to help us with anything we needed. We went down to the showroom, had dinner and drinks, and then Paul came on stage and started singing. I cried. He was so professional, so fantastic, and I had always loved his voice, his songs so much a reminder of my past and the music I loved. He sang all my favourites: "My Way," "Diana," "Having My Baby" and, of course, "Put Your Head on My Shoulder." He even invited Michael up onstage to sing with him, introducing him as a protege that he and David Foster were working with.

"Watch out for this kid," he told the audience.

Afterward, we went backstage for a special reception. We ate from a wonderful buffet, where all the serving dishes and cauldrons were copper, and then Paul decided we would all go gambling in the casino. I love the slots, so I declined when Paul asked if I wanted to play poker at his reserved table. Once they were seated, I went over and put my arm around Paul's shoulder and kissed him and told him how much everything he had done meant to us. He said: "Think nothing of it. But what are you going to do?"

I told him I was off to play the slots, and he took my hand and put a chip in it and said: "Go have some fun." I put the chip in my pocket, because I had to go to the washroom. When I took it out afterward, I saw it was a $500 chip. I was shocked, and I took it back to Paul and told him I couldn't accept it. He argued a bit, then sighed, took it back and gave me one for $100: "How's this?" he asked. I said, "That's better," and off I went. I played the same quarter machine for several hours, so long that my ankles were swollen, and left with $107 in my pocket. Later, when I got back to our room, Michael and Debbie gave me a hard time. They had gone looking for me, couldn't find me anywhere and were worried that I had been swallowed up by Sin City. But we all sat down, had some wine and laughed about it.

The next day, we met Paul for brunch, and when I tried to hand the $100 chip back to him, he smiled in amusement and said: "Don't insult me." So I kept it.

In July, Michael flew to Victoria, David's home town, to perform at his annual David Foster Foundation fundraiser, alongside Ed McMahon and Jay Leno. That September, he also performed at the Kodak Theatre in Hollywood and was back in Vancouver for the Burnaby Arts Council Cavalcade of Stars event.

Meanwhile, all that good food we had been eating every day during the CD sessions and our Los Angeles socializing had come back to haunt us. One day, we were in the kitchen in our apartment, and I looked at Michael and said: "We're both getting fat." He agreed, and when I said that I was seventeen pounds heavier than the day we landed in L.A., he confessed to being about twenty pounds heavier than usual, which was saying something because he not only always worked hard to stay slim, but whether we liked it or not, he was in a business where looks matter and where thin is in.

So we decided to do something about it. I started cooking more vegetables, we began eating more salads and, like everyone else in L.A., we went on a protein diet. David went on the same diet, and he was pleased we were planning to drop a few pounds, because he had noticed our collective chubbiness as well.

As soon as I decided to get back in shape, I realized I was getting a bit lonely, so I signed up for a local online dating site and met this nice fellow, who looked like a teddy bear, which I always liked. His name was Larry, and he was divorced and in the cosmetics business with his son. He travelled a lot but was based in L.A. Meeting him was great motivation to lose the weight, and three weeks after I began the diet, and began talking to him online, I had lost fourteen pounds.

I finally agreed to meet Larry for dinner. We went to a trendy seafood restaurant along the Malibu strip. We hit it off instantly and dated for several weeks. Then he had plans to move to Florida for his work, and since I would be eventually moving back to Vancouver, we decided that a long-distance relationship would be too challenging. We stayed in touch for several months.

CHAPTER SEVEN

Calling All Agents. And Bruce Allen.

It was time to get serious about finding representation for Michael. It had been something of a bone of contention between us from the moment Michael had started getting high-profile jobs, especially when he started to get noticed outside of Vancouver. Now that he was making a CD with David Foster, and superstars like Paul Anka were in his corner, it was becoming even more important for me to find someone I could work with, someone who had more connections and more industry savvy than me, to take Michael where he needed to go in the next stage of his career.

It wasn't as if I hadn't been trying. I had already interviewed several respected managers but had no luck convincing them to take us on. But, with David's support behind us, the doors were opening a lot faster.

One day, during the summer of 2002, David had said to me, "There's someone I'd like you to meet," and off we went to see Caresse Henry, who was Madonna's manager and had also managed Ricky Martin and Jessica Simpson. She was friends with Madonna's long-time publicist, Liz Rosenberg, who would also become a good friend. "She'd be a perfect fit to work with you," David said, and when we got to the Beverly Hills Hotel, where we were meeting her for lunch, it wasn't long before I knew he was right. I loved her, we all got along so well and she was very keen to work with us.

Michael was happy, too.

One night, the four of us—Caresse, Liz, Michael and I—went to dinner at the Ivy. We sat on the patio, and it was magic. I knew I had found the perfect person.

Caresse said there was a lot of work to do, and she thought we could forge a relationship. She would get me started on some little public relations projects, she said, getting profiles out on Michael and so on, and see where it went. She would tell me what to do, and I would do it. It sounded like a good plan, and I was never so happy. This is what I had always wanted. For me, this was it.

A few days later, Caresse phoned and said: "Beverly, why do I feel like this is not going to work? I think it's going to be time-consuming. I don't think Madonna's going to be happy with it." She wasn't sure she was going to be able to work with David, she said, for reasons that she didn't share, but I was heartsick. And she asked me not to tell Michael or David why.

I was devastated. "Oh my God, I can't believe you're saying this. This is the worst thing you can say to me."

David and Michael were just coming back from the airport. They had been at an out-of-town event, and when Michael called me from the car, I told him the news. He was shocked. I told him it had something to do with her schedule with Madonna and left it at that.

Michael told me later that David turned to him in the car and said: "I can't believe it. Maybe she doesn't want to work with Bev."

Later, at home, Michael wanted to talk more about it. I told him I didn't know what her reasons were, and he repeated what David had said: "But, Bev, what else can it be? Think about it."

He was furious, madder at me than he had ever been, the first time, really, that I can remember him being truly angry with me. I couldn't really blame him for being mad, because he deserved to know. It was his career, after all. But I couldn't tell him.

He started to shake: "Do you know? Do you know how close you are? You're this close," and he held up his thumb and index finger.

I said: "To what, Michael? To firing me?"

"I don't know," he said, "but you're this close."

I was getting angry, too. I asked him what exactly I meant to him, what my role was.

There was a long pause, and still shaking, he said: "I'll tell you what you are. You are my safety net."

I went into my bedroom, to cool off, and when I came out later and walked into the kitchen, I said: "Michael, I'm leaving."

He smiled, because he was already over it, and said:

"You're not going anywhere, and that's final. You are not leaving. Believe me when I tell you, you are not leaving."

"I am," I said. "Because right now, I feel like I have no dignity."

I was so angry, and hurt, and upset that after all we had been through, he didn't trust me enough to just let it go.

So I decided to sleep on it. The next morning, I was in the kitchen making coffee when Michael came out of his room and said: "Bev, you know you're not going."

And I looked at him and said: "No, I'm not going."

"Michael," I said, "it is not because she can't work with me. So let's just chalk it up to 'she's busy.'"

And he let it go.

Also that summer, on another recommendation of David's, I booked an appointment to see Dan Cleary, who was Natalie Cole's manager. I met him in his office. He was a quiet, conservative man but very receptive. We talked about his relationship with Natalie and about what he might do for Michael, whose work he admired. I told him that I had interviewed several managers and had several more to see, and we left it that I would get back to him with a decision.

Dan was lovely, and said all the right things, that he would love to work with me, but I always wondered what he and the other managers I talked to had thought that really meant, because I knew, and had been told by people like David and Paul, that it was unusual to have co-managers in the kind of set-up I was envisioning. Normally, one manager would take over from another, so I knew that all these respected people in the business were probably looking at me and thinking, "Well, I already have a secretary."

Of course, David was always working on something, and the new *Spider-Man* movie came out that year and was a huge hit, so he wanted Michael to take a crack at the movie's iconic theme song. He sent me to the local record store to find the original recording of the song so that he could get Michael to vocally recreate the trademark sound effect—the swoosh of slinging webs. I couldn't find it, but he took Michael into the studio and had him do his own take on it (which was released as a single titled "Spider-Man Theme" in 2004 and, although it wasn't part of the soundtrack, was played during the credits of *Spider-Man 2*). And then David decided that Michael would sing their version of the *Spider-Man* song on September 14 at a fundraiser in Chicago for McDonald's World Children's Day.

It almost didn't happen.

Michael and I had made a return trip to Vancouver in September to visit our families just before the Chicago concert. Lisa was pregnant with my first grandchild, and she threw a big party for me. I regaled everyone with all my crazy Paul and David and Los Angeles stories, and told them all about the recording sessions. My family and friends were thrilled for me, of course, and it was over all too soon before I had to head back.

I wasn't back in L.A. long before I got a call from Michael, who was on his way to Chicago when he was stopped at the border by U.S. customs. He had been back and forth between Canada and the U.S. too many times for work, and they didn't care that he had applied for a working visa and was still waiting for it to be issued. They wouldn't let him leave Canada. In Chicago, the man who hired him for the event got on the phone with his lawyer, who must have had some kind of clout, because they managed to find out where Michael's application was in the U.S. customs system and had it approved immediately. Michael was on his way.

Josh Groban was also playing the McDonald's event, and he was there with his manager, Brian Avnet. David was there, too, and when Michael called to tell me all about it, like he always did, I could tell that he was frustrated. Everyone else in the show, he said, was there with their representative, and he had no one.

"Bev," he said, "it's embarrassing."

My heart sank. But I knew he was right.

Two weeks later, Michael and I flew to Las Vegas, because Michael was performing with David at the Grand Slam for Children concert fundraiser for the Andre Agassi Charitable Foundation. There was a black-tie dinner, a live auction and, of course, the concert, which attracted more than six thousand fans to the MGM Grand Garden Arena.

Along with Michael and David, the performers included Elton John, Martina McBride, Dennis Miller, Robin Williams, Carlos Santana and surprise appearances by Jamie Foxx and Rod Stewart. David, for the seventh year, was the event's musical coordinator, and when the weekend was over, close to $6 million had been raised for Agassi's charity.

At one point, Bruce Allen, who had been rejecting my managerial advances for years, was at a press conference panel with his client Martina. Michael and David and I were in the audience, watching. Afterward, Bruce, who had seen Michael rehearsing, went over to David and started chatting with him about Michael and the CD, and David said to him: "Bev is over there."

So Bruce came over to me and shook my hand, and I said, picking up from where our last conversation had left off: "Well, Bruce, what do you think? We've got this CD, and I'm still looking."

He asked me to send him a copy of the CD, which was finished but hadn't been officially released, and I did. A few days later, after he was back home in Vancouver, he called me.

"Beverly, it's Bruce Allen. I listened to the CD. I give it a nine."

"How come you don't give it a ten?"

"I never give anybody a ten. We should talk about it."

Not long after, he was heading to Nashville and stopped in Los Angeles. We met at his hotel, sat in his room and started talking about everyday stuff, his life and my life.

I began to press him about taking on Michael, but he played hard to get. "I've never done anything like this before, and I'm getting too old for this," he said, by which I knew that he meant it would be a lot of work taking on another act, and that he wasn't sure how it would work, this co-managing arrangement that I wanted.

I wasn't convinced by his protestations. "Well, I'm older than you."

"That's good," said Bruce, grinning, "because you can do all the work."

We went for lunch, at a diner he had heard about

that served the best hot dogs in L.A., which turned out to be Pink's. I loved that, because he could afford to eat anywhere he wanted, but instead we went for hot dogs, big, delicious hot dogs, served on paper plates.

Over those hot dogs, we talked about Michael, and I told him of the struggles we had been through and our search for representation, and he told me about how tough the business was. He called me Michael's "secret weapon." It was a light-hearted lunch and a quick chat, because Bruce never sits still for long, and we didn't really make any decisions.

I told him that I was still interviewing other managers, but I knew in my heart that he was the one. He was tough and straight, and that's what Michael needed. And he was from Vancouver. I just knew he was the perfect choice, but I had always thought that.

On David's advice, I had made an appointment with Arnold Stiefel, who was Rod Stewart's manager. It was October by then, and we met at his office and began to chat. He asked if he might phone Michael directly, and I said of course, because I was never threatened that someone would steal Michael away.

So, he called Michael and, in the course of the discussion, asked him: "What are we going to do with Bev?"

And Michael, who told me about the conversation later, said to him: "What do you mean?"

Arnold was up front: "Well, Michael, if I work with you, I fly solo. I don't do this, you don't do this in the industry, taking somebody on like this."

And Michael, who knew that Caresse had said she'd work with me and that Dan and Bruce had seemed okay with it in our preliminary discussions, said: "Well, you know what? If you can't see the value that she can bring to you, then you wouldn't be the manager for me."

Arnold later called and told me of their conversation and said it wasn't going to work, and I thanked him for his frankness, and that was the end of our dealings with Arnold.

Michael and I then met with Marty Erlichman, who was Barbra Streisand's manager. He was older, business-like and soft-spoken. He was all about the music, and he talked a lot about the music with Michael, which Michael loved. At one point, when Michael was out of the room, Marty told me he was willing to manage Michael. But, tell-ingly, he never said he'd be willing to work with me. I just knew, after we left his office, that he was a solo act, too.

But, back in the car, Michael was excited and turned to me and said: "That's it. He's the one I want. He knows about the music. Look what he did with Streisand. He's the one. That's the manager I want."

He went on and on, and when he realized I was being unusually quiet, he said: "Okay, what's wrong? You're not saying a thing."

"Michael, he's too old for you. He's older than I am, and I'm too old for you."

I told him that Marty and Barbra clearly had a different kind of manager-client relationship—Marty had discov-ered Barbra and had always been her manager, rather like Michael and me, but we needed a different kind of energy to take us into the future.

Michael said: "Okay, I know what you want. You want your Bruce Allen. Okay, you know what? We'll go with your Bruce Allen. But if it turns out that it doesn't work, it's going to be your fault."

It was a concession, a big one on Michael's part, but the decision was made.

I said, only half-joking: "It's okay, because I always get blamed for everything anyhow, and why should this be any different."

And so I called Bruce and said: "It's official. I want you as his manager. So what do we do now? And Bruce, do we have to live in L.A.?"

And Bruce Allen, my new co-manager extraordinaire, said: "Hell, no. Nobody should live in L.A."

I could have kissed him.

Meanwhile, David hadn't given up on Warner Bros. Even though, with all his clout, he couldn't convince them to take on Michael, he had managed to get Michael an appointment with company president Tom Whalley. David told Michael he was to go alone, without me, and do his best to convince Mr. Whalley why Warner Bros. should sign him.

On October 23, I dropped Michael off at the Warner Bros. lot and went for a coffee nearby, waiting and fretting over what they were talking about and how it was going. This was huge, and I prayed it would go well.

It didn't take long before I saw Michael walking back. My heart was in my mouth.

He sat down and said: "Here's how it went. Tom Whalley said to me: 'Michael, why should I sign you? We have Sinatra on Reprise.' I said the only thing I could think to say. I said, 'With all due respect, Mr. Whalley, Frank Sinatra is dead.'

"And I told him. I am not Sinatra; I am not any of them. I love all of them, but I am me. Nobody sings the music like I do now. And the new generation is ready. They're ready for these songs, because it's the music that everybody loves, because no matter how old you are, it always comes back. And I am that person. I grew up with that music, and it burns inside me."

He said Tom Whalley told him he would give it some thought, but I could tell that Michael didn't really know what to think about his chances.

And then Michael did something that, at first, upset me. He looked at me and said: "You know, Bev, you are a very smart woman. You rode this all the way, knowing that the day would come when you could see the light at the end of the tunnel. You're a very smart woman."

It took me aback, because he made it sound as if I was only in it for the promise of some kind of payoff.

I told him that I didn't know whether to cry or slap him. "Have you not been there, Michael? Are you a stranger that I'm telling a story to?"

It was the first time he had ever truly hurt my feelings. I didn't think of my decisions as being smart. I never knew what was going to happen. I was with him because I believed in him, because I loved him as if he was my own son. He could see that I was upset and said: "No, no, you were smart. You were there."

Michael, in all the years we had been together, had never said a mean thing to me, had never uttered anything unkind about me to anyone, even when I frustrated him, even when he was disappointed, and I don't know why I bristled at his comment. Perhaps it was because of my own insecurities about my lack of managerial capabilities, but over the years, I have come to realize it was probably just Michael's way of acknowledging that even though I always said I didn't know what I was doing, I knew that one day he would be sitting across the table discussing his music career with the president of Warner Bros.

A few days later, I was in our apartment, with Michael's grandfather Mitch, who was visiting, when the phone rang. Michael was downstairs working out in the building's gym.

I answered, and David said: "Bev, are you sitting down?"

I thought, Oh my God, this is it. I knew right away what he was calling about.

"Warner Bros. went for it," he said. "They're taking him. Tom Whalley went for it. They're going to sign him."

And, of course, I started crying. "Oh, my God, David. Oh my God."

I hung up, and by then Mitch was crying, and we both headed down to the gym to tell Michael. He was totally engrossed in his exercising, along with another man in the room.

"Michael," I said, "you're not going to believe it."

He looked at both of us, his weeping manager and his teary grandfather: "What?"

"I just got off the phone with David, and they went for it. They're going to sign you."

He could only say, "Oh my God."

And, ever the gentleman, he turned to the other fellow in the room and said, "Do you mind? I have to leave," to which his exercising partner, who by then had figured out what was going on, replied, "No, of course not. Congratulations."

The three of us went back upstairs and started to call everyone we could think of, and of course, nobody was home, which always seemed to be the way when we had good news. But when we did eventually get them all, everyone just cried because they were so happy.

We had done it. We had a David Foster–produced CD, a crackerjack new co-manager in Bruce Allen and, now, a recording contract with Warner Bros.

It was almost surreal.

There was barely time to catch our breath before we had to get down to business. David had recommended a terrific lawyer, Peter Lopez, and he and David and Bruce ushered Michael through the actual contractual process, which would take some time. I left it to them but made sure they would tell me the moment it was signed, because, I told them, I needed to know it was a done deal.

Meanwhile, at one of the meetings we had begun having with the reps from Warner Bros., it was strongly suggested that Michael change his name. They didn't like the name Bublé and wanted to change it back to Santaga, Michael's mother's maiden name. They thought it was a nicer name, for some reason. It was funny, because Michael's parents had also discussed the same thing with me, back when I first started working with him. I told them that I liked the name Bublé and that he should keep it.

So we all went around the boardroom table and discussed the pros and the cons of the two names, and when it came to Michael, he said: "You know what? Seven years ago if you had come to me and asked me this question, I might have had a different answer. But my name is Bublé. People have learned how to say it and learned how to spell it. And I'm not changing it."

It was an emotional meeting for me, though I don't really know why. Perhaps because it was such a big deal, to be sitting there helping make major decisions about Michael with Warner Bros., perhaps because I knew it was all coming to an end, that this was it for me. That I had taken him where he needed to be, and now I needed to step back and let the pros take over. I kept welling up, and all I could think about was a conversation that David had had with Michael not long before, when he told Michael, "Bev needs to stop crying."

But I couldn't help myself.

I thought Michael's answer about his name was

A special VIP parking space for Michael and me at Warner Bros. Studio in Los Angeles.

brilliant, and the Warner Bros. folks seemed to accept it, and that was the end of the debate.

Then came the photo shoot for the album cover. Warner Bros., of course, was picking up the tab, and it was decided that the backdrop would be a fantastic glass-walled house up in the hills, overlooking Los Angeles.

It was sunny and many of the indoor shots were taken at different angles to take advantage of the light. One shot had Michael leaning against a wall inside the house, wearing a pale blue crewneck sweater, with the sun shining like a halo around him. Other frames had him in a suit or lying on a bed wearing an open-necked white shirt. Outside, they dressed him in a black zipped sweater and sports jacket with jeans. The session took all day, but the photographs, by a New Yorker hired by Warner, were superb.

When the proofs were ready, the project head called Michael and me to come in and help with the decision on the photograph that would be used for the CD cover. It was a fun task, but it was tough, because there were hundreds of shots to choose from. I was pleased when the final decision was left to me, perhaps because I knew Michael better than anyone in the room, and I didn't hesitate for a second: the sunny shot with him in the blue sweater. Michael laughed and said: "Boy, that was fast. Are you sure, Bevy?"

I was sure. And even though it ended up being just the headshot on the cover, it was still the right choice, perfectly capturing Michael's twenty-seven-year-old boyish charm and maturing handsomeness.

Bruce and I were on the phone with each other a lot at that point and had already decided that he would come down, in November, because with the recording contract now signed and with him now on board, we needed to find Michael an agent.

When Bruce got to L.A., the three of us began the rounds of every major agency in town, including the three big ones: William Morris, Creative Artists and ICM.

We were wined and dined by all three, and each of the firms came to the boardroom table fully prepared, with their executives, marketing people, sales people and tour people all on hand, because David Foster and, now, Bruce Allen were involved, and this was serious business.

They talked about everything they could, and would, do for Michael. There was no talk of money, of course, because we all knew the industry standard dictated that their take would be 15 per cent of whatever jobs they booked for him.

Bruce, of course, would then take his management fee. Also deducted would be all of Michael's expenses, right down to the couriers and photocopies and Bruce's travel expenses. A $250,000 job, for instance, could end up as a cheque for Michael somewhere in the mid-$100,000 range, after all the commissions were paid out and the expenses deducted.

Back in our Westwood apartment, on the same day we had seen the William Morris people and had pretty much exhausted our search, Bruce suggested that the three of us go back to the apartment to discuss things. He and I sat down at the dining room table, and he told Michael to sit on the couch "so you don't cheat," and I got us each a pen and paper. Bruce told us to write down the names of the agencies—one, two, three—in order of our personal preference.

We did, and he said, "You done, Bublé?"

We compared notes. Bruce and I had chosen William Morris as number one, but Michael had picked the agency as number two.

Bruce laughed and said: "And that's why you're not looking after your own career."

William Morris it was.

To know Bruce, of course, is to love him. He is tough and smart as a whip, both charming and bombastic, and not given to keeping things close to his chest. When he has something to say, he says it, usually without a lot of sugar-coating. He would become my rock, but I know we were oddballs as far as he was concerned. When he walked into our place that day, it suddenly hit him just how close, and unusual, my relationship with Michael was.

Or, as he put it, looking around: "Jesus, so you really do live with him. I've never known a manager who lives with their artist."

He didn't get it, but he thought it was cute.

We went out to dinner to celebrate our decision, around the corner to the Palomino, which was one of my favourite spots to stop for a martini after a long day. We had the chopped salad, which was a big thing in L.A., because everyone was on a diet, and it was a wonderful evening.

I left it to Bruce to work on Michael's behalf with the William Morris Agency, and from then on, he handled everything else.

In mid-November, Lisa—who was pregnant with her first child—and her husband, Mike, came down for a visit.

Daniel and his girlfriend, Kelly, to my delight, had also moved to Los Angeles that year, after Daniel, who had graduated from aviation school and had spent nearly three years in Seattle working as a flight instructor and building flight hours, landed a job flying Learjets. Kelly was studying law at USC, and we saw a lot of each other during the time I was there.

To have us all together made for a great little family reunion, and I wanted to share with them some of what I had been up to, so I called David and asked if we could come by his house so that I could show my kids the place where Michael's CD was recorded. He told us to come right over.

And wouldn't you know it, on the way to David's house, we got a flat tire. I called David, who said he was sorry that he had to leave, but his assistant would let us in. We fixed the tire and headed through David's big gates, and my kids were overwhelmed by how beautiful his estate was.

At one point, my son-in-law said to me: "So, how do you like the traffic here?"

"Oh, it's not bad," I said, but before I could say another word, Lisa piped up jokingly: "No, when you have a Town Car picking you up at 12 o'clock from Westwood and taking you to Malibu, and you don't leave Malibu until 11 o'clock every night, the traffic is probably just really great."

She was always so amused about what she thought was

my jet-set life and loved to tease me about it, but I knew she was happy for me.

At the end of the month, Bruce came down to Los Angeles and we talked some more about how Michael would be managed. I was so pleased with him—he was absolutely the right choice for Michael.

It was strange, perhaps, that Bruce and I never seemed to talk about money, or how I would be paid. I don't really know why, but it was just something we didn't get into. It was too early in our relationship, and was still completely uncharted territory, for Bruce and for me.

And we didn't talk much then about what I would do, as Michael's co-manager under Bruce's tutelage, once I was back in Vancouver. Michael told me later that when he and Bruce were chatting alone one day just after we hired him, Bruce said to him: "What are we gonna do with the broad?" And Michael said, "Well, I'm going to keep her. She has been loyal and worked hard all this time."

Bruce was pleased with his answer, Michael said, because it gave him a sense of the maturity and generosity of the young man he had just taken under his wing.

"I'm really glad you said that," he told Michael, "because I would have wondered what kind of person I would have been working with if you hadn't."

Not long after Bruce took on Michael, he told me later, one of the Sony bosses called him and expressed his surprise that Bruce had agreed to manage a lounge singer from Canada. "I can't believe you're doing this. I can't believe you're taking on this kid. I think you're making a mistake," he said. Many months later, when *Michael Bublé* hit 500,000 copies sold, I phoned Bruce and asked him if he called his friend back to tell him we had the last laugh. He chuckled.

Suddenly it seemed like everything had come together for Michael and me, a perfect storm of hope and hard work, perseverance and serendipity. The CD was done. Warner Bros. had signed him. The details of the contract were being worked out. The photo shoot was done. And we had finally found our manager and a top-notch agent. Michael was over the moon about it all; it was the happiest I had ever seen him.

He had found his holy grail. And, in a way, so had I.

It was time for me to go home.

I told our lawyer, Peter, that even though I was going back to Vancouver for Christmas, I would return to Los Angeles, because the lease on our apartment wasn't up until March, and besides, I couldn't leave L.A. without knowing that Michael's contract had been signed, sealed and delivered. A few days later, a delivery came from Paul for Michael, Debbie and me. A large chest with the MGM logo on it, which I still have, was full of goodies, and one of my gifts was a beautiful round, domed crystal candle holder.

Before I headed home for the Christmas holidays, David's assistant called to invite us to a holiday party at Tom Whalley's house. Michael didn't want to go, though, because he didn't get an official invitation. He was in a snit about it. "Where's my invitation? What's this? A last-minute thing? We're not going."

Debbie and I were sitting in the apartment, trying not laugh about it, while Michael was out on the patio pouting, having a cigarette and a glass of wine. He kept opening the patio door, poking his head inside and saying, "And Bev, we're not going. You know, Bev, you think I'm kidding, but we're not going." And the door would close.

I turned to Debbie and said: "Go get ready." She smirked and went to have a shower.

The patio door opened again. "Bev, you think I'm kidding. I'm not kidding. We are not going to that party. Really, seriously, Bev."

He closed the door. I went to get ready, Debbie was ready, and then Michael came in, went to get ready and never said another word about it.

Soon we were driving up a long lighted driveway to the valet parking stand in front of the Whalley mansion, surrounded by the cars of the stars—Jaguar, Rolls-Royce, BMW and many a Mercedes-Benz. We were still driving our leased Nissan, which embarrassed Michael, but I didn't care.

The home was gorgeous, festooned with lights and decorations. Inside, the party room was completely white, from the walls and lights to the carpet and furniture. There were high chrome tables and stools, and food stations lining the walls around the room, serving an incredible assortment of seafood, meat, cheeses, mini-burgers, gourmet macaroni and cheese, and too many desserts to count.

There was even an ice bar, which I had never seen before: a bar made entirely of ice, standing about three metres high with a built-in ledge that held rows and rows of martini glasses. I stepped up, helped myself to a glass and asked the bartender, who was standing on top of the counter, for a lemon kiss. He mixed the cocktail, poured it through a hole in the column of ice and it tumbled down, ice cold and ready to sip, right into my glass.

I, of course, had to immediately find a quiet little corner so I could phone Lisa: "Oh, my God, you can't believe it," I gushed, which I always did any time we went to one of these swank events, or any time I met someone famous, which seemed to be every other day.

She was so happy for me, and I was so happy to be heading home for Christmas. I knew it would be good to take a breather, be with my family and see my old friends.

By then, everyone had heard about our good news and knew that, after all our struggles and setbacks and the many bumps along the way, Michael and I had finally made it.

It had taken nearly ten years, since the day we first met back in 1993, but we had made it.

CHAPTER EIGHT

What Do We Do with Bev?

As much as Michael's life was about to change, as much as he was on the threshold of the kind of superstardom we had only dreamed about, so, too, was my life about to take a turn.

I was blissfully home in Vancouver, as 2002 wound down, on an extended Christmas visit with my family. I had never really celebrated Christmas after I had converted to Judaism, but I had always said that the kids could do whatever they wanted when they got older. Both of them had studied Judaism when they were younger. Daniel kept the faith but to this day doesn't practise it, and he and Kelly celebrate Christmas. Lisa stayed true to actively participating in all the Jewish holidays, but Mike isn't Jewish, so the Bishops do Christmas as a family.

Over the holidays, I was on top of the world, so happy I could squeak, which is what I always used to say to my kids when I thought my life was perfect. And at that moment, it was: my son's career was flying high and he had a lovely girlfriend, Kelly; I was moving back to Vancouver; my daughter was pregnant; Michael and I had accomplished everything we had set out to achieve all those years before; and, recalling the discussions Michael and I had had about money, I knew—on the eve of my sixty-third birthday—that I didn't have to worry about my retirement anymore.

I had always been good with money, always had some savings, even during the many lean years, but much of my working life had been contractual, and my career in the entertainment business had not exactly provided the kind of benefits that would yield much of a pension beyond the standard amount provided by the federal government to all Canadian citizens when they reach age sixty-five.

That Christmas was one of my best ever. I was staying with Mike and Lisa in my old place on Fourth Avenue. Lisa had been working in marketing and sales at an agency but was on leave awaiting the arrival of the baby. Mike was bartending, about to land a job at Sysco Vancouver, a food service distribution company. It was a position that capitalized on his experience in the hospitality industry, something he learned working with his parents and two brothers in the family-owned Sea Breeze Lodge on Hornby Island off B.C.'s coast.

When I wasn't catching up with them and spoiling my very pregnant daughter, I was visiting old friends I hadn't seen in ages. I reconnected with Ray, with whom I had stayed in contact during the year I was away. Things were okay between us, and I knew he was happy for me.

I was going back to Los Angeles to celebrate New Year's Eve. I had a date and wasn't about to miss it. After

Larry had moved back to Florida, I was once again alone in L.A., so I had logged back on to the website where we had met and dove into the online dating scene again.

I met a really nice widower named Stephen, a massage therapist who lived in San Francisco. He was so good-looking, with a moustache and beautiful blue eyes. He was a great dresser, too, and I liked how he looked on his profile, so I contacted him. We went out for dinner, to a beautiful place in Santa Monica, and saw a few movies, before I left to spend Christmas in Vancouver. I was so charmed by him that, when I got back home, I immediately called up his profile and showed it to Lisa and all my friends.

Stephen had made special plans for us to celebrate New Year's. He had good friends in L.A. who were away for Christmas and offered him their home to stay in. He wanted to surprise me, and when we got to the house, he had a beautiful dinner ready, a dinner that he had cooked himself. The food, and his company, were terrific. He introduced me to tequila, good tequila, Patron, and we laughed and talked and had a wonderful time.

The next day, when we were out having breakfast, my phone kept lighting up with David's number. When I finally answered, David said Josh Groban was looking for a backup singer and thought the woman who had sung "Lady in Red" in a one-off recording session he'd had with Michael might be a good choice, and he needed her number.

I said, "David, to be honest with you, I'm kind of still on a New Year's Eve date." He laughed and said, "Okay, call me when you get home." I did, but it turned out that a violin player was chosen to tour with Groban.

Stephen knew that my L.A. lease was up in March and that I was moving back to Vancouver, so even though we really liked each other and stayed in touch for a time after New Year's, we both understood that it was pointless to pursue a long-distance relationship.

I was in Los Angeles when my son-in-law, Mike, called to say that my grandson, Taylor, the new light of my life, had arrived on January 22, 2003. He was beautiful and healthy, and I was so thrilled, because as old-fashioned as it might sound, I always thought that when it comes to having children, you should start with a big brother.

I immediately headed back to Vancouver, and a few days later, Michael sang at Super Bowl XXXVII in San Diego, one of the performers on an entertainment bill that included fellow Canadians Celine Dion and Shania Twain, along with Beyoncé, Sting, Carlos Santana and Bon Jovi. It was one of Michael's first appearances that I really had no involvement in.

At that point, Warner Bros. was still working on the details of its five-CD contract with Michael, as well as a separate contract with David regarding *Michael Bublé*, to ensure that David recouped the money he had ended up spending out of his own pocket to make the album.

Michael also got an advance when he signed the contract, and David made sure I got 15 per cent of that, which was a nice little bonus. It made me think of a conversation Michael and I had, just after he signed with

Warner Bros. He said: "Bevy, what are you going to do with all your money?"

And I replied: "Michael, we don't even know what that looks like. But what's more important to me than the money is that I get to revel in the glory that we have worked so hard for. That I get to be there when it all happens."

On February 14, 2003, three days after the CD release, Michael appeared on *The Today Show*, with Katie Couric. Michael called me from New York, as he always used to

Michael recording at Warner Bros. Studio.

whenever he was away, and said, "It's a good thing you're not here, Bevy. The weather's terrible."

The release of *Michael Bublé*, bolstered by the marketing and promotion arms of Warner Bros., Bruce's connections and Liz Rosenberg's publicity machine meant an avalanche of exposure for Michael. He appeared on the NBC soap opera *Days of Our Lives* and *Live with Regis and Kelly,* and his story began showing up in *People* magazine and dozens of other media forums.

He was everywhere, and he was happy. And so was his family.

I never said a word to Michael, or anyone, about how crushed I was that I wasn't in New York or involved in the other promotional appearances. I know Michael didn't exclude me on purpose, and I know he wouldn't purpose-fully do anything to hurt my feelings. He was just on a different trajectory, playing with the big boys, and they were guiding him now.

And so I prepared to move home.

Before I left Los Angeles, David, Linda, Paul, Michael and I, along with some other friends, had a nice going-away dinner at our favourite Greek restaurant, the one we frequented almost every day during Michael's CD sessions at David's studio. It was a fun night, with lots of food and booze and conversation, and I was happy.

Michael was getting ready to go on tour, and David had arranged some alternative accommodation for him, so he had to move his things out of the apartment the same day I did. Our lease was up on March 1, but it was a building favoured by celebrities (Michael was always pointing out La Toya Jackson in the parking garage), and the rules seemed a bit flexible, which worked in our favour, because they hadn't rented our apartment right away and let Michael stay for a few days after the move.

On the day of the move, though, Michael was so distracted by everything else going on in his life that he had left the packing to the very last minute, until the moving trucks were literally on the doorstep, and then it was a mad scramble. He was schlepping his things out little by little, a lamp here, a bag of clothes there, and it was hilarious to watch. Finally, the truck was full and the movers headed north with our possessions, mine going into storage and Michael's to Debbie's parents' home in Tsawwassen, where they unloaded everything in the driveway and nobody even knew what was in the boxes.

I said goodbye to David, and to Los Angeles, and flew home to Vancouver on March 15, with one suitcase, because I was going to bunk on Lisa and Mike's couch until I figured out what I was going to do, and because Lisa jokingly informed me that I could only bring one suit-case, my big purple one. I was okay with that, because I was so happy to be home. And my family was so happy to have me home.

Taylor was my new obsession, a perfect baby, and I cherished every minute I spent with him. I would sleep on the couch in the living room, right beside his bedroom, and every morning, as soon as I could hear him stir, I would get up and hang out with him until Mom and Dad started their day.

I loved it. I stayed on that couch for seven months, spending my mornings watching cartoons with Taylor and getting reacquainted with my old life. Lisa was still on maternity leave, Mike was in his new job at Sysco but still bartending evenings, and we all got along really well.

Every night, after Lisa, Mike and Taylor had gone to bed, I would put Michael's CD on the stereo, which was right beside the couch where I slept, and listen to his beautiful voice in the dark and relive everything that had happened in the years we had spent together, all that we had been through, the ups and downs, the laughing and the crying, the triumphs and the disappointments. I played that CD so much, I practically wore it out.

I had been home a month or so when I finally popped in to see Bruce at his office on East Pender to discuss the co-managing arrangement we had talked about when I had originally asked him to represent Michael. Bruce was always nice to me, so receptive and respectful, and this time was no different: "Beverly, if you want, you can bring your computer and set up a little office in my boardroom." On one of those visits, I asked Bruce if I could take him to lunch. He said that he didn't usually leave the office for lunch, but perhaps I could pick him up a No. 2 cheese-burger meal at Wendy's, with a Coke. I said: "Diet Coke?" "Hell, no," he said, "none of that diet shit. Just a real Coke."

But Bruce really didn't give me anything to do, and neither of us seemed to know exactly what it was that I would or could do, but he was insistent about trying to get me on board. "Bublé wants you involved," he said, "so you can come here."

I told him I would think about it and went home. And I did think about it and realized that there was really nothing for me to do. The reason I had wanted Michael to work with Bruce is because Bruce had the industry experience, the connections, the established reputation and a crackerjack operation that could do for Michael what I couldn't. The truth was that his staff was already doing all the work that I might have done for Michael. Bruce was trying to tell me something when he said to me one day, while we were still trying to figure out how I fit into the equation: "Beverly, why don't you just go to the spa and enjoy yourself. Haven't you worked your ass off?"

But it was a wonderful summer. Lisa, Mike and Taylor were away on Hornby Island for most of it, and I was going to the local gym in Kitsilano several times a week and had never been in better shape. When I wasn't working out, I was lunching and hanging out with old friends.

In advance of his tour, Michael continued to perform, including a week-long run in mid-April at Feinstein's at the Cinegrill, a new nightclub at the Hollywood Roosevelt Hotel. I flew down to see the show with my buddy Vance Campbell, and we sat in the audience with Bruce and Debbie. David was there with his group of friends, too, all of us cheering on our boy, whose CD had already gone gold in Canada.

The next day, I met Bruce downstairs in the hotel—after getting lost looking for the lobby where I was supposed to meet him, which annoyed him—and joined him for a meeting with Warner Bros. Later that night, Michael called me and said Bruce and I needed to talk about money, because "we're moving along" and he was still unsure how the "co-managing" was going to work between Bruce and me, or even how the discussions

Michael and I had had about money translated to reality now that he was tied to Warner.

It was all a bit fuzzy, which I know was as much my fault as his, and I don't know if Michael was just repeating what he had been told by his parents, or Bruce or David or Warner Bros., or other people who had been counselling him, but one thing was clear: Michael wanted me to call Bruce and sort it out.

I went to my hotel room, sat on the bed, picked up the phone and called Bruce in his room.

"Hi Bruce, this is Bev, and Michael said we need to talk."

"Well, yeah, yeah, yeah, we do, but I don't even know, and it's very confusing for me."

I agreed, because I felt the same way: "This is something you've never done before, isn't it?"

"Yeah," said Bruce. "In the industry it's unheard of to take somebody who's managed somebody and start working with them. I'm only doing this because Bublé wants you on board. So we need to talk about this when we get back to Vancouver."

The next morning, I was having breakfast with Vance. I told him there was something I wanted to talk to him about, discreetly. I had always trusted him, and we had become good friends since our days at BaBalu.

Vance said: "Are you going to talk to me about the conversation you had with Bruce Allen?"

"What?"

"Yeah, I heard part of it. I was coming back to my room after having a drink. This is what I heard. I heard you say to Bruce, 'So Bruce, I don't know what that looks like, because obviously you've never done this before, have you?' and then I went into my room."

So we chatted about it, and Vance told me not to worry, he knew that no matter what happened, Michael would never let me down.

I flew home, and decided to start going to meetings at Bruce's office to see how things were being done with regard to Michael. Bruce's assistant would call me, tell me what time to be there for a meeting and I was. I was impressed with Bruce's organization. Everything was so professional, so businesslike.

At one meeting, Bruce's accountant lined up all the paperwork pertaining to Michael's account on the board-room table, pages and pages, showing all the expenses, all the fees, everything.

Not long after that meeting at Bruce's office, Michael's dad, Lewis, called me and said it was time for us to have a meeting, that he would be looking after Michael's money from then on, and we needed to sort things out.

"Bev, we don't need a lawyer," he said, and I agreed, because I didn't think we did. We had always had a great relationship and I knew that they would treat me right. There had never been trust issues between Michael's parents and me. It was as if I was a member of the family.

I wasn't worried.

Not long after, I met with Lewis for a coffee at Starbucks. I turned over several bankers boxes that pertained to the business, and we discussed compensation for the years I had spent guiding Michael. We agreed that the terms would remain private, and my professional break from Michael seemed complete.

And then, in July, came the Commodore concert. Bruce had asked me, on a previous occasion, if Michael could sell out the Commodore Ballroom, an iconic Vancouver art deco music venue renowned for its springy dance floor. "Of course," I said. It was only a thousand seats, and his star was on the rise following the release of his CD: he had performed with Chris Isaak, contributed two songs for the movie *Down with Love*, sang with his band at the famous Blue Note Jazz Club in New York's Greenwich Village and did a sold-out show at the Winter Garden in Toronto.

The Commodore? In his hometown? No problem.

Michael's publicist and my old friend Liz Rosenberg came to town for the Commodore concert, and she invited me to come out for dinner with her and Bruce.

Bruce was talking with Liz about the presentation of some plaques at the Commodore concert, and I couldn't help myself. I asked him if I was going to get a plaque, too.

"Bev," he said, "just go to the concert and have a good time."

There was a huge lineup to get in. I saw lots of friends and agency people I knew as I walked around in the crowd. I was so proud of Michael, so proud of what we had done, hugging everyone and feeling like I owned the world.

At some point during the night, in a backstage ceremony, the band members got individual gold record plaques, with their names on them. They hadn't even played on the CD, but they got gold records. Bruce got one, too. But not me.

A few days later, I called Michael and asked him,

outright, if I was getting a plaque. He said yes, and not long after, I got my plaque.

But it had become clear, crystal clear, that I was no longer a part of the Michael Bublé story.

It was hard enough getting used to that, and it didn't help that I ran into reminders of my diminishing importance around every corner. I would get emails and phone calls, from everybody I knew and everyone who knew my story with Michael, from friends and musicians and people in the industry, and they would say, "How come you're never mentioned in all these stories?"

I had another taste of my new reality with the *W5* interview.

W5, a respected, long-running current affairs show on CTV, had called to say they wanted to interview me, along with Bruce and Michael, for a piece about my years with Michael and my managerial hand-off to Bruce. They would be conducting separate interviews, they said, and mine was to be done in Mike and Lisa's place, where I was still living. I was thrilled.

The day came, the cameras were all arranged and the interviewer, a woman, sat across from me in the living room and asked me a series of what I thought were thoughtful questions: how did I feel being with Michael all those years, how did it feel to hand him over to Bruce and so on. They took shots of me and panned over to the gold record plaque, and I was so excited that I was receiving some public recognition. Better yet, it was television and it was my story!

Amber saw the show on satellite before I had a chance

to see it and called me: "Bev, Bev, the interview with W5 was just on, and it was just great."

I said: "Oh, how did I look?"

"What?" she said.

"Well, you know, my portion."

"Bev," said Amber, "did you have a portion?"

"Amber, Amber, they were at my house, we had this big interview."

I had been cut entirely from the show. It was too much. I broke down on the phone and cried.

Amber immediately called Michael and told him that I was upset about the show. He called me and said: "Bev, I don't know what to say to you." I could almost picture him using his hands to signify weighted scales as he tried to explain: "Bev: Mulroney wedding/Beverly Delich. Mulroney wedding/Beverly Delich. Bev, what do you think?"

I was inconsolable: "But, Jesus, Michael, they came to my house, and they asked me all this stuff, and that was important stuff, that I turned you over to Bruce, and I even told her that I was the one that picked him."

He didn't know what to say.

Amber didn't either. The few conversations we had at that point were different than those we had shared over the years. We had never talked about things like money, because ours had always been a more intimate connection about the latest crazy antics of "our son." But as the disconnect began, that once-easy discourse was becoming difficult. At one point, I told her I was having trouble with the transition, but I realized I couldn't really tell her why.

Amber tried to commiserate, but it was just as hard for

her. On several occasions, she would call and let me know that Lewis would be dropping off some boxes of stuff for me from Michael, things such as calendars, specially packaged CDs and other memorabilia.

By mid-October, sales of *Michael Bublé* had gone platinum.

CHAPTER NINE

Coming to Terms

*I*t was time to get my own place.

I couldn't stay with Mike and Lisa forever, and I was still living out of that one purple suitcase. There was a great building down the road from their condo, called Spyglass Place, and in January 2004, I rented an apartment on the second floor, with a deck facing south. I loved the location.

It would be the first of several moves I would make over the next few years, as I settled into post–Michael Bublé life.

I still spent a lot of time with Taylor—he was a year old at that point—because Lisa was back at work and Mike had started his new job. I had a new car, Lisa and Mike's Honda Accord, which I loved, because it was in great shape.

And then, two days after I moved in, my apartment was burglarized. The enterprising crook crawled up the latticework trellis attached to the condo below me and squeezed into a window I had left open. I came home and noticed that my bedroom door was closed, something I never did. My heart sank. I didn't go any farther but instead went down to get the building manager and asked him to come in with me.

As soon as I walked in, I knew that my computer, which I kept in the bedroom, would be gone. And it was. And with it, my electronic records, my contact lists, my email lists, my correspondence, photographs, appointments, important dates and details of events. Everything. Luckily, I had it all on a backup USB, but it bothered me that all of that information was in the hands of a stranger. And, of course, I still had my bankers boxes full of videos and DVDs and other Michael-related memorabilia that were untouched, which was a relief.

Michael was never far from my thoughts. I was following his career from the sidelines, a spectator now, instead of an insider, instead of a daily confidante. I kept track of his tour and his appearances and all the publicity that had followed his CD release, and despite the loss I felt because of our disconnect, it was all a great source of pride for me, if somewhat bittersweet.

That spring, Michael invited me to join him and his family at the Juno Awards on April 4 in Edmonton. He suggested I go with his sisters, his grandparents and his mom and dad, who were making all the arrangements.

In Edmonton, Bruce went with Michael to the live show at Rexall Place, but the family and I stayed behind in the hotel room having pizza. It was a little awkward, because I had been feeling so left out, but I never let on because I didn't want them to be sad or embarrassed on such an important night. I just enjoyed the evening for what it was.

Michael had been nominated in the categories of Album of the Year and New Artist of the Year. He won the latter but lost the former to Sam Roberts. He called the hotel room to let us know he'd won, and we were all so thrilled for him.

And I realized, in that moment, that it had been exactly ten years since I had run into Michael outside that restaurant on Granville Island and, remembering his performance at the Big Bamboo talent show, decided then and there that he needed to enter the 1995 PNE talent contest.

And now, he was on the national stage, accepting his country's highest music honour.

And I was getting back in the social swing of things. It was great to see all my friends and business contacts again, and we all picked up right where we left off. One night, I was at a summer garden party at a friend's place in Richmond, and Marit and I had had a cocktail or two when she turned to me and said: "Do you think Paul Anka would like my dress?"

Marit, like me, was a big Paul Anka fan, and she always wore the cutest clothes, and for the party she had chosen an adorable sleeveless dress with little clotheslines all over it. I lost it and began laughing. But I had my cell phone in my purse, and I still had Paul on my speed dial, so I said "Let's just see," and I called him. I got Paul's voice mail and left a message: "Paul, this is Beverly. I'm at a party in Vancouver, sitting next to my best friend, and she has on the cutest dress you can ever imagine, and she loves you with all her heart, always has; in fact, she may be your number two fan, because you know I'm your number one fan. And this dress is so cute, and I know you can't see it, but she just asked me if I thought that Paul Anka would like her dress. Paul, would you call her and just say hello to her?"

I left him Marit's telephone number and hung up.

The next day, he called her: "Marit, this is Paul Anka calling. Beverly said you had on a lovely dress last night, and I'm sure I would have liked it." Marit was delighted and called everyone afterward to tell them all about it. It was such fun for her, but I wasn't surprised, because I knew that Paul would call. He's such a class act, so much so that when he came to Vancouver for his November 13, 2004, concert at the Centre for the Performing Arts, he gave me eight complimentary centre-row tickets and told us to stay in our seats after the show. We did and were soon escorted backstage to visit with Paul and take pictures.

A class act.

Since I had been back, I had also reconnected with Ray, who had been suffering since 1987 from colon cancer and kidney problems but was always such a showman that he continued performing, even while dealing with his illnesses. He was beginning to fail, though, and even though we weren't as close as we once were, he was still a good friend, and I tried to spend as much time with him as I could.

In February 2005, I moved again, this time to a lovely apartment above Pier 1 Imports at Pine and Broadway, one of my favourites of all the places I have ever lived. It was the best spot for me, because it was on the west side of town, and because I could just walk out the door and everything was right there.

And then came the news that spring that Lisa was pregnant. We were all ecstatic, and we were all hoping it was a girl so that Taylor could have a little sister. She and Mike hadn't wanted to know the baby's sex when they were expecting Taylor, but this time they did, so when the time came I went with Lisa for the ultrasound. She told the technician not to tell her but to write the gender on a piece of paper, and on the way home in the car, she handed me the paper and said, "You look at it, but don't tell me, because I don't want to know until I go home and share it with Mike. So, look, but don't say anything, and no expressions."

So, I did. I opened it and looked at it and didn't say anything or even make a face, and she just kept driving. But I was so thrilled.

Mikayla Josephine—her middle name was after my mother—was born at Grace Hospital on November 9. I stayed home with Taylor so that Mike could be with Lisa during the delivery, and when they phoned me to say that she had been born—beautiful and healthy with a little patch of hair—I instantly loved my little Miki-Jo, which I immediately nicknamed her.

I had two grandbabies, and I was so happy I could squeak.

But as new life came along to brighten our lives, so, too, did more sad news.

My old friend Hugh Pickett had also been sick. He'd

One happy family: My daughter Lisa, her husband Mike, and my adorable grandchildren Mikayla and Taylor smiling for the camera in 2010

had cancer of the bladder for years, though he never talked about it, being far too proud and far too private. As he got sicker, he also began to suffer from dementia. I would go see him at his lovely Shaughnessy house, and we'd be talking about different things we had done and sometimes he would completely lose track of our conversation or substitute one name when he meant another. It was sad to see. His partner, Gord, had hired a caregiver, and he was in good hands, but I knew that we didn't have much more time to spend together, so I made the best of every visit.

Hugh died on February 13, 2006. He was ninety-two and had lived such a full life and had done so much to put Vancouver on the entertainment industry map, and I knew we would miss him so. His memorial, fittingly, was held at the Orpheum Theatre, where he had introduced Vancouver to so many great acts, and Gord asked me to be one of the guest speakers. I was honoured, because our friendship had meant so much to me. I really loved him.

It was hard to lose Hugh, but it was easy to share what we'd had together. The place was packed, with old and young, with entertainers and friends and people in the arts and music business. I talked about how lively and colourful and direct he was, and about his undeniable flair and his spot-on gift for identifying talent, which had so aptly earned him the title of impresario, of Mr. Entertainment. I talked, too, about how he came to be a judge at the PNE, and how the first time we heard Michael sing at the PNE talent show, he knew—everyone there knew—that this was a star in the making.

And I talked about the special relationship the three of us had, including this anecdote: Once on a visit to Hugh's home, he took us down to the basement filing cabinets and showed us the contracts of some of the entertainers he had booked through the years. We had many a good chuckle at the fees for a top performer back in the '50s and '60s. As we were leaving, Michael turned to Hugh and said: "I noticed that you don't have any security at your home." Hugh said: "What would they take?" Michael and I looked at each other at the same time and said: "Everything!"

He was the best, and I still miss him.

Ray's health was continuing to decline and I knew, too, that we would soon be losing him. He was hospitalized on several occasions, and at one point, I sent for his daughter, Kim, a nurse who lived Montreal, and she came out and spent some time with him and worked with his lawyer, sorting out her dad's personal affairs.

One day I got a call from one of his students, who had my name from a contact list Ray had kept when I was in L.A. She said: "Beverly, I think Mr. Childs has died. I came for my voice lesson today, and the housekeeper had already found him."

It was April 5, and Ray had died in his sleep. He was eighty-two. There was a police constable there, and I asked to speak to her, and when she confirmed that Ray was dead, I phoned Kim, who immediately flew out to Vancouver with her mother.

Ray was cremated, and I planned a memorial for April 18 at Rossini's in Kitsilano, a favourite restaurant of Ray's. It was really beautiful. Sibel Thrasher, who had been Ray's first friend when he came to Vancouver, sang a lovely tribute. Michael was there, too. I told the story of how Ray and I had met, and how much he had meant to all of us.

I talked about his two aliases—he was Leroy Childs in the U.S. and Ray Carroll in Canada—and how he always lived with such hope and such a positive outlook.

I talked, too, about how we had been together through good times and bad, how we comforted each other during our trying times with cancer and how, in our twenty years as friends, he had valued my honesty and directness as much as I admired his tenacity and sense of humour.

It was hard losing two close friends, so close together.

I hadn't been at the Pine Street apartment much more than a year when I decided it was time to invest in some real estate. In June 2006, I bought an apartment in a brand new high-rise close to Lisa and Mike.

In August, Daniel and Kelly got married in an intimate wedding ceremony in Everett, Washington. Gabriel's band played at the reception, just as they did for Mike and Lisa, and it was nice to have them accompany me on "True Love," which I sang in honour of the newlyweds. It was a fun celebration and, as only mothers can, I convinced Daniel to breakdance, which he had always done when he was young. Embarrassed as he was to be breakdancing at his own wedding, he did it. And he was great, even though he ended up having to go to a chiropractor on his honeymoon.

It turned out I would stay in my new condo only a year, and it was all Lisa and Mike's fault, but in a good way.

They had bought a beautiful townhouse near Commercial Drive and wanted me to move into a place right across from them. It had become available, with a year-long lease, because the owners were travelling.

"But, Lisa," I protested, "I just moved into my place." She thought that was a silly excuse, because she wanted me closer to them.

I mused about it for a bit and, of course, finally gave in. I signed the lease, rented my condo to a lovely couple and moved to the Commercial apartment in 2007. I would end up staying there for the next three years.

I loved living across from the Bishops, because it allowed me to be so much a part of my grandchildren's daily lives. Every morning, I would go over and make coffee for Lisa and me, and breakfast for the children. I taught my grandchildren how delicious toast can be when it's dunked in coffee. I gained weight, of course, because often Lisa would bring me leftovers, which I would eat after eating my own dinner. Because my deck was bigger than theirs, Mike brought over his barbeque and would cook their meals on it, socializing with all our neighbours.

In January 2007, I joined the entire Bishop family for a fourteen-day Caribbean cruise, a wonderful way to celebrate Taylor's fourth birthday. There were fourteen of us altogether, and along the way, we spent three days in Disney World in Florida. We ate, swam, ate some more, and I gambled in the ship's casino with Mike's brothers. Mikayla was still not walking, so it wasn't a very relaxing time for Lisa, but I was always happy to have a little nap with the kids to give her a break during the day.

I was sixty-seven and in good health. I was enjoying my retirement and my precious time with the Bishops, my son and daughter-in-law in Seattle and my family in Montana.

One day, in the fall of 2007, Michael was in town with his then-girlfriend, actress Emily Blunt, and suggested he and I meet for lunch at Provence, a restaurant close to his Yaletown condo.

It was the first time I had sat down with him for a quiet conversation between just the two of us, in the four years since we had come home from Los Angeles.

I decided this was the time to be honest with him, to share some of what I had been feeling: "Michael, I never wanted to say this to you, because you've been busy with your career and I don't want to make you feel guilty, but because you and I are so close, I have to tell you this."

He looked at me. "Okay, what is it?"

So, I told him. I told him that when I came home, it killed me that I was swept aside, and that the feeling just wouldn't go away, and that anybody who ever knew about us never let it die, always reminding me that I never got any press, that I wasn't written about anywhere, that I wasn't in the *W5* interview.

And then Martin van Keken, who had booked Michael years ago when we were working in Vancouver, walked by and waved, and Michael said, "Hey, look, there's Martin."

So, Martin came over with a friend and they sat down, and the dynamic of our lunch completely changed. Our private conversation was over. When Martin got up to leave, Michael did the same, saying he had to get going. We hugged and parted. I was disappointed that I was never able to finish my personal conversation with Michael.

A few months later, nearing Christmas, I was chatting with Michael on the phone when he said that he had made a great deal of money that year, and he was giving each of his musicians a generous bonus for Christmas. I said to him teasingly: "Does that mean my Jaguar is going to be in the driveway this year?"

He paused and said: "Bev, what are you driving?"

I told him I was driving a Honda Accord.

Just before Christmas, I was getting ready to go to Montana to visit my brother and sister when Amber phoned me and said, "We need to get together, because Michael has a little gift that we need to give you."

I was delighted that she had called and said I really wanted to see her but wondered if it could wait until I got back from Great Falls, but she insisted—"No, no, you know our boy"—so I said okay, and we arranged to meet, along with Michael's sisters and grandmother Yolanda, a few days later for lunch at Milestones in Port Coquitlam. Michael was away, not yet home for the holidays.

I kvetched to Lisa that day that it was a long drive, in the pouring rain, but she told me just to go and enjoy myself. And I was looking forward to seeing Amber, Crystal, Brandee and Yolanda again. I realized how much I missed them, missed having them in my life and talking to them about "our boy."

During lunch, Amber handed me a beautifully wrapped package. It was a special limited edition of Michael's latest CD, *Call Me Irresponsible*. Inside the package was a cheque for $50,000.

I had all but forgotten the conversation I'd had with Michael, having left it to him to do whatever he was going to do when he remembered to do it, so I wasn't expecting this.

I was over the moon.

We had a wonderful lunch, though I couldn't help but notice they were all spending a great deal of time on their cell phones. And then Brandee said: "Bev, could you do me a favour?"

She said that her husband, Rob, wanted to buy a used car, but she wasn't sure about the one they had been looking at, and she wanted an unbiased opinion, and it was nearby, and would I mind? It never occurred to me that it was an odd request. We finished lunch, and Brandee said she'd drive me over to look at the car.

Brandee and I pulled up to a nearby car dealership,

and so did the rest of the family. We all piled into the showroom and started looking at the cars. We walked all the way to the end of the showroom, and I didn't even notice the salespeople following us or that we were being videotaped.

And then I saw it: a shiny, champagne-coloured Mercedes-Benz with a big red bow around it.

Amber turned to me, put out her hand and said: "Bev, here's your keys." I looked at the keys and at her and said: "No, Amber, I've got my keys."

She said it again, and I repeated that I had my keys, even though my car was still back at the restaurant, and then she smiled and said: "Bev, this is your car. It's from Michael."

And, of course, I cried. I was speechless. I couldn't believe it. I hugged every one of them. They made me get in the car, to try it out for size. I could barely see because I was crying so much, but it was beautiful, a brand new 2008 four-door Mercedes c300 with leather seats and wood-grained detailing. Beautiful.

I was beside myself with happiness, and not really thinking straight, so I asked the manager if I could come back the next day to pick it up.

"I'm in no shape to drive this home," I blubbered. He said, "Of course." I managed to compose myself enough to purchase the insurance so that I could drive it away without any fuss when I returned.

On the way home, I phoned both Lisa and Daniel to tell them the news and discovered that everybody—all my family and friends—already knew about it. Brandee had made sure everyone was in on the surprise, which was so

Michael would become a Grammy Award-winning artist, selling millions of CDs and performing around the world. RICHARD DREW/CANADIAN PRESS

wonderful. The next day, Mike drove with me to the dealership and I picked up my little beauty, only I was a little nervous about driving it, so I asked him to drive it home, which he didn't mind at all.

That night, Lisa, Mike and I took the kids to the Keg for dinner, and we were sitting at the bar having martinis, while Taylor and Mikayla munched on raw veggies and dip. I was so happy I could squeak.

I was on top of the world.

A few days later, I called Michael. He was just coming into town, and I was just heading to Montana, and I thanked him and said: "Who does this?"

And he said: "Well, who does what you did?"

My financial adviser, of course, thought I should sell the car and invest the money, along with the $50,000 cheque. I said no way. I told him it was more than just a new car and it meant something to me, because it had come from Michael. I told him I was keeping it. Forever.

Lisa agreed: "Mom, you should be driving a Mercedes."

It took a while to get used to it, though—in fact, I had the car for a few days before I would even drive it. Lisa and Mike insisted I take it for a spin before I left for my holidays, so I drove it around the neighbourhood for a bit. It was smooth and sleek and fast. I loved it. And when the kids asked if they could drive it when I was away, of course I said yes, so Mike used it to deliver Christmas gifts to his clients, and Lisa took it to show off to her friends at the radio station where she worked.

And I got a lot of mileage with the story during my holiday visit with my brother and sister and their families, who were delighted with my good fortune. It was so wonderful to see everyone whenever I visited Montana, and over the years we tried to make sure that the distance between us didn't keep us apart.

I always marvelled at how close Jerri and Robert and I had grown over the years, considering we had been brought up in such a strict, non-communicative house-hold. But maybe that's why, maybe we were making up for those lost years. Whatever the reason, we cherished spending time together, whether they came to visit me in Vancouver or I flew to Montana. Both had adult chil-dren of their own, of course: Jerri and her husband, Bill, had four kids from his previous marriage—Karen, Jenny, David and Kathy—and Robert and his wife, Ruth, had three: Tara Sue, Danika and Delena. And there were plenty of grandchildren to keep us all busy. Robert had been struggling for some time with Parkinson's disease, but we always had such a good time when we got together, and they were thrilled when I took them all out to dinner in Great Falls and told them it was "on Michael Bublé."

As 2007 gave way to a new year, my life settled into a routine.

And then, one Saturday, in the fall of 2008, just home from a visit with Daniel and Kelly in Seattle, I noticed that I kept feeling that I had to yawn, that I was short of breath. It was a strange sensation. The next day, I also started to feel like my blood pressure was going up. All of it began to scare me, so I went over to Mount St. Joseph's Hospital. My heart was pounding, and I was panicky. They took my blood pressure, which was too high, and put me on oxygen and started doing tests.

The doctor on duty decided to send me for a stress test, which was tough, and I didn't pass. I needed a cardiologist. I was assigned to Dr. Singh at MSJ, and he told me that I suffered from atrial fibrillation, which is a common form of heart arrhythmia, or irregular heartbeat, increasingly prevalent as one ages. It's caused by abnormal electrical activity in the upper heart chambers, which can cause the heart to quiver instead of contracting normally. Kind of like a faltering battery. And because it shuts the heart down, if only for a few seconds, it can cause blood clots.

Dr. Singh put me on medication, but right off the bat, it didn't agree with me. My peripheral vision wouldn't work, and it petrified me, so I called an ambulance, but when I got to the hospital, they told me it was a normal reaction and would clear up after a few hours.

It did, and my heart settled down.

I was sixty-eight and, technically, retired, but I still had Silver Lining Management and wanted to continue doing what I'd always loved. So I began working with several local vocalists as a consultant, which had always been my favourite part of the business.

About the same time, Michael asked me to check out a young singer he had been collaborating with named Erin Boheme, who was already signed with Concord Records in Los Angeles and was working on a CD. I went down to visit her and thought she was good, and she really wanted to work with me, but the geography was, again, an issue, and my thoughts were slowly turning to other things back home, so we decided it just wouldn't work.

I was thinking even more seriously about writing my book—something I had always wanted to do—and had begun a journal many years earlier, so I started visualizing what it would look like. Even though I knew I wanted it to be a memoir, I gave a lot of thought to what would go in it, what it would say about me, and my life, and my time with Michael.

I was also travelling a bit, to see family in Montana, of course, as well as friends in Los Angeles and Toronto. As often as I could, I took off to New York, one of my favourite cities.

Daniel and Kelly often came up to visit, and I frequently drove down to Seattle. They had settled into a beautiful home and life as a happy career couple, he still flying Learjets, she working as a lawyer. There were no children, but they doted on their pets—three cats and, eventually, a rescued greyhound they adopted after one of the cats died at a ripe old age. The time I spent with them was different than the time I spent with Lisa and her family, and I loved going to see them, because we had such a great time together.

So, as if I was starting anew, I moved again, this time back to my favourite part of town: the west side.

My new pretty brick-covered three-storey condo in the South Cambie area, which was bright and modern and big enough for Taylor and Mikayla's sleepovers, suited me perfectly. It was just a short stroll to grocery stores, restaurants and coffee shops, and a short jaunt over the Cambie Bridge to meet friends downtown. The drive to Lisa and Mike's was less than ten minutes.

That July brought sadness to the family, with the death

from heart failure of Jerri's husband, Bill. When she called us to let us know he wasn't doing well, Daniel and I drove down to Great Falls to be with her, and were able to spend some time with him during his last hours. They had been married for thirty-four years and had a wonderful life, but it was a tough time for us all.

In the fall of 2010, I went on a luxurious Mediterranean cruise to several ports of call in Spain, Monaco, Italy, Greece and Croatia. I was seventy, my health was good, I had my wonderful family and I was feeling great about life in general.

Early that November, a friend and I went for dinner at Don Francesco's. It was one of my favourite restaurants, because I felt at home there. We had a lovely dinner and headed down to the underground parking garage. I got into the car and went to put on the seat belt, when I realized I couldn't feel the buckle. Suddenly, I felt a quivering in my jaw and tried to say "oh, hell," but nothing but gibberish came out. I was slurring my words, and I could hear it, and it scared the hell out of me.

"Oh my God, a stroke." I mumbled the words.

And then, just as soon as it had begun, it was over. I was able to put on my seat belt, and by the time we pulled out of the parking garage, I was talking again.

It had lasted only about ten seconds, but I knew it wasn't good. We drove to the emergency ward at Vancouver General Hospital.

I was in the hospital from 9:30 that night until the next morning. Lisa came to stay with me, and I had all kinds of tests throughout the night. At 5:30 a.m., the doctor came in and said he was pretty sure it was a transient ischemic attack, or TIA.

It was, in laymen's terms, a mini-stroke.

The doctor arranged for me to connect with the Heart and Stroke Foundation, and he put me on blood thinners. Back home, I tried to get back to doing normal things, but I was so unsettled, even more than when I had breast cancer. I didn't know if, or when, it would happen again.

I've always been proactive about my health and taking care of myself, about doing the research on the things that have ailed me and taking the medical advice given to me. I started going back to fitness classes, doing cardio exercises and making sure I stayed in shape.

On December 9, I was at home talking on the phone with my son-in-law, Mike, when it happened again. I started garbling my words, and it lasted for about five seconds.

"Oh my God, Mike, did you hear that?" I asked, after it had passed.

He said yes and told me to relax. Again, I was off to emergency, where the doctors checked me out and determined that it was another TIA. My cardiologist prescribed a newer medication, one that had just come to Canada, a top-of-the-line blood thinner. Once I started on the new medication, I began to feel more confident and relaxed.

In February 2011, I joined the Bishops in Maui for a vacation and started to feel like my old self again.

When I returned home, I ran into Bryant Olender, who had played piano for Michael all those years ago, and who had been away from the scene dealing with personal issues. But now he was back in Vancouver, trying to kick-start his music career.

It was so great to see him, but I didn't think much more of it until I received an email from him not long after our encounter. He asked to meet for coffee. He had met a successful businessman who thought he was a talented singer and offered to bankroll a CD, but only if Bryant was serious enough to find someone to represent him, someone professional.

Bryant knew I still had the Silver Lining Management Company and wanted me to be that person.

I told him I would think about it. I needed to know that he was truly sincere about his ambition, and a few days later, I went to see him play at the Pan Pacific Hotel lounge. His benefactor was at the show, and we talked about Bryant, and his talent, and we agreed that I would work with Bryant. He asked me to do a budget for the CD, and I did just that, detailing the cost of a producer, the recording sessions, my fees and even the wardrobe that Bryant would need for the CD and publicity photos.

Bryant went into the studio in April 2011 to record the CD. It was like being back in David Foster's studio with Michael, when I would go with him every day and hang on every detail. It was fun and exciting to once again be part of realizing someone's potential.

In June, Michael was in town and I asked him to do me a favour, to listen to Bryant's CD, *So Strong*. He was always very busy when he was in town, so I was pleased that he agreed to meet with Bryant and me. We met at the Warehouse Studio in Gastown, where acts such as Elton John, Bon Jovi, Elvis Costello, Bryan Adams, Avril

Lavigne, Nickelback, Alanis Morissette and Motley Crüe have recorded their music, and fittingly, both Michael and Bryant had recorded some of their tunes there.

Michael listened to the entire CD and afterward said: "Bev, it's a real CD. It's beautiful. It's not canned, and Bryant is more talented than I remember." Bryant was thrilled, and so was I.

Joined at the Heart

*I*t was an invitation like nothing I had ever received, a white square box wrapped in a fine white mesh bag, hand-delivered in a specially wrapped package to my front door.

The tag, addressed to me and a guest, had a delicately scripted capital B embellished with crystalline rhinestones. Inside the ribbon-wrapped silk-lined box were two note-cards, one asking guests to respect the bride and groom's request to refrain from taking photographs or recording any of the evening's festivities, the other detailing accommodation and parking information, including instructions for free valet parking.

The actual invitation inside the box was gorgeous, softly padded and wrapped in a pretty white ribbon with a rhinestone buckle. It read: Michael Bublé and Luisana Lopilato cordially invite you to join them in celebrating their recent marriage.

The date and time were set for Friday, May 20,

2011 at 6:30 p.m. at the Pan Pacific Hotel in downtown Vancouver, "for cocktails, dinner hors d'oeuvres and dancing all night long."

I had been expecting the invitation, because Michael had mentioned it was coming in a phone chat we'd had earlier. He and Luisana had formally married on March 31, in Argentina, in Luisana's hometown of Buenos Aires, where she is an actress and model. He told me there was going to be a big bash in Vancouver for his friends and family back home—it was their third wedding celebration and would come after their three-week Italian honeymoon—and his mom and sisters were doing all the planning, and, he laughed, "I don't even know who's going to be there."

Lisa and Mike got an invitation, too, as I knew they would. They had been along for the ride all those years and not only adored Michael and his family as much as I did, but Lisa had remained good friends with Brandee, and she and Mike knew it would be an unforgettable evening and a big Vancouver event.

Michael was having one of the best years of his career, maybe of his life. Not only had he married Luisana and settled into their beautiful home in the Hollywood Hills, but on February 13, he took home his third Grammy Award, this time for Best Traditional Pop Vocal Album, for *Crazy Love*. He had more than a dozen hit CDs under his belt, was working on a soon-to-be chartbusting holiday album, *Christmas*, and even wrote a book, titled *Onstage, Offstage*. With 35 million records sold worldwide, writing credits on some of his best-selling records and a Top 10 ranking as one of the globe's top-grossing live tour acts, he was at the very place we had always dreamed he'd be.

I couldn't have been happier for him.

Lisa and I immediately went shopping, to find something dramatic but not too over the top to wear. I went to Holt Renfrew but couldn't find anything, so I ended up at Ashia Mode, a little boutique on Granville Street. I said to the sales clerk: "Do you have anything over a size two?" and she laughed and assured me they did. I told her it had to be something dressy, something I could wear afterward. Nothing prom-dressy but classic and comfortable. I told her it was for an event a few weeks away, and we got to talking, and eventually I told her it was for Michael Bublé's Vancouver wedding reception. We picked out the perfect outfit: long black crepe culottes and a white linen jacket with a Queen Anne collar. Lisa lent me a chunky crystal necklace, and with my black pumps, I was set.

And I was so thrilled for Michael, happy that he had found Luisana. I had always made a point to keep out of his private life, even though we were so close and, especially when we lived together in Los Angeles, it was hard not to know what was going on in each other's personal lives.

And I knew that, at times, it was difficult to juggle a serious relationship while trying to build a career, especially a showbiz career. And, in Michael's case, career was everything. The long distances and the times apart simply take their toll, no matter how hard you try, and it was no different for Michael.

He and Debbie, who met in 1996 while doing *Red Rock Diner*, were together for eight years and were even briefly engaged. Their breakup, in November 2005, was a difficult one. She was a sweet, vibrant young woman, and they had been so good together, so much in love. He had written his huge hit "Home" for her, and she appeared in the music video for the song, and when their relationship ended it rocked them both.

And when his much-publicized engagement to British actress Emily Blunt—they had met at an Australian awards show in 2005—ended badly in July 2008, Michael was devastated. He had written "Everything," a hit in 2007, for Emily, and theirs was a high-profile relationship, so the entertainment press had a field day when they split. In an interview with CTV in October 2011, Michael said that, in hindsight, the breakup had, oddly enough, been good for him. He had been "reckless with other people's hearts," he said, and it had forced him to change.

I had met Emily only once—the three of us joined my son-in-law Mike for lunch at the Sandbar on Granville Island, where they arrived on Michael's Vespa scooter—and she was lovely and gracious, telling me that Michael had told her wonderful things about our time together and she was glad to finally meet me.

With the news of his November 2009 engagement to twenty-three-year-old Luisana, I knew that, at thirty-four, Michael had family and possibly kids on his mind, and I was delighted for him.

Meanwhile, I was thinking more and more about the book. People were always saying to me that I should write a book, because of the ongoing changes in my life, my conversion to Judaism, my years in the interior decorating business and the Vancouver entertainment industry, my eleven years with the PNE youth talent search and, of course, because of my time with Michael.

You've had such an interesting life, they'd say, for a

small-town girl from Butte, Montana, and you discovered Michael Bublé. There's a book in that, Bev, they'd say, and they were right.

Amber had encouraged me, too. In the early days of Michael's career, when she and I were so close, and talking constantly about Michael and all the craziness, she always used to tease me: "Put this in your book, Bev, save this for your book."

And now, nearly eight years after returning from Los Angeles and adjusting to my new life, I was ready.

Michael had come into my life when I was fifty-three, at a time when I might otherwise have been looking toward retirement, but even after all the ups and downs, I have been grateful for every minute of our time together.

Along with my own family, my kids and my grandchildren, Michael has been one of the highlights of my life.

He had always known that I wanted to write a memoir. I told him that it wouldn't be a "telling" book, that there wouldn't be anything in it that would affect anyone's career or reputation, that it was about my feelings and my life, and about our time together, but it was also going to be a chronicle not just of the good times but of the tough ones, too.

He would listen and then say, perhaps to reassure himself: "But it will be about your life and your marriage to Al, and your kids and all that stuff, right?"

When I started thinking about what would be in the book, I began contacting some of our old colleagues, because I wanted a special chapter featuring a few of the key people in his career. I wanted them to write about their role and what they remembered. And when I asked them to contribute, I mentioned, jokingly, that there would be no censorship.

One spring day, Michael and I met for lunch at a little eatery in Kitsilano. We sat down in a booth and weren't even there for five minutes before he blurted out:

"Bev, there's something I have to talk to you about. I heard that you're going to have a section in your book where people get to say whatever they want, completely uncensored."

"Oh my God, Michael, who told you that? It's not going to be that at all. It was a joke about being uncensored. Do you think I would let people write stuff without editing it? Besides, since then, I've decided not to have that chapter, because I realized I would just be leaving out too many people."

He asked me again what the book would be about and whether it would be about my life.

"Yes, Michael. And it's also going to be about our time together."

He didn't say it in so many words, but I think it made him nervous.

"Look, Michael," I said, "it's going to be about my feelings, about how I felt my whole life, about me."

He nodded, and we didn't talk about it anymore, instead chatting about his Crazy Love tour and his upcoming Vancouver party.

May 20 arrived. I started the evening at Lisa and Mike's, enjoying a vodka and grapefruit cocktail or two, and then we took a taxi to the Pan Pacific.

David Foster and his date were getting out of the car at the same time we arrived, and I was so happy to see him.

We hugged, and I'm sure the photographers were slightly annoyed that I might be getting in their way when they were trying to take pictures of David.

We took the escalator up to the ballroom, but Lisa and Mike and I decided to stop for another drink in the lounge, where I ran into Michael's aunt Libby. It was so great to see her. We hugged, and it immediately put me at ease.

We finished our drinks and then headed for the big ballroom where the party was being held. The guest list numbered five hundred, and the lineup was starting to get long. When we got to the door, the hostess took our cell phones, put them into little white boxes and handed us tickets, like coat check stubs, so that we could collect them later.

The ballroom was glorious, decorated to the nines, and almost everything was white. There were white tufted leather couches and white flat-screen televisions and mirrored tables, urns of roses and orchids, silk-covered walls and crystals dangling like sparkling streamers from the ceiling. There was even a cupcake lady wearing a huge white dress layered with five tiers of white cupcakes, self-serve dessert on the move.

The whole thing had such an elegant and posh 1940s vibe. It was exquisite. It was so Michael.

The first person I saw was Yolanda, Michael's grand-mother, so I went over to her and gave her a hug, and we both got a little emotional.

And then Mike tapped me on the shoulder and said: "There's Amber and Lewis."

I walked over and hugged them both and said congratulations.

It was a wonderful night, and it was so great to see everyone, not only Michael's family but also David, Liz Rosenberg, Vance Campbell, Bruce Allen, Michael McSweeney, Gabriel Hasselbach and Humberto Gatica. They were all there, as well as so many other people who had been with Michael and me from the beginning.

Michael married Argentinean model and actress Luisana Lopilato in 2011.
NATACHA PISARENKO/CANADIAN PRESS

When Michael and Luisana, so gorgeous and radiant, made their entrance—he in a dark Hugo Boss suit, she in a white beaded silk gown—it was magical. I made my way to him and gave him a big hug and my congratulations. I was so proud and so happy for him.

Michael gave a sweet speech, and when he thanked Bruce and then thanked me—"Bevy, for all that she did for me at the beginning, and all our time together"—it felt good to be recognized. It was the same feeling I had all those years we spent together, as if we had always been joined at the heart.

And then, as though my glass coach was about to turn into a pumpkin, I knew it was time for me to go. I had seen everyone I had wanted to see, said everything that I had wanted to say, and the night couldn't have been any more perfect.

Just before midnight, I told Lisa and Mike I was ready to leave, but they should stay behind to enjoy the party. I picked up my gift bag, which held a little treasure chest full of Hershey's Kisses and a special white-jacketed EP featuring four songs: "Feeling Good," "You're Nobody 'Til Somebody Loves You" "The Way You Look Tonight" and "Haven't Met You Yet," which was the hit single Michael had co-written and released in 2009 for Luisana.

I took the escalator back down to the lobby and hailed a cab. When I got home, I hung up all my clothes and went to bed, visions of the evening, of my life, dancing in my head.

I felt like I could fly.

Index

Photographs indicated in **bold**

Royal Jelly Orchestra, 117
Royal York Hotel, 118
Russell, Sylvia, 51

Santaga (grandpa), 145–46
Science of Mind, 52–53
Serbian Orthodoxy, 23
Shapiro, Robert, 152
Siegel Entertainment, 70
Silver Lining Management, 77,
    144, 220, 224
Singh, Hari, 91
Sitel, 121–23
Smith, Lyvia, 48
Smith, Scott and Shannon, 112
"Spider-Man Theme," 171
SS Media, 112
Stanley Theatre, 102
Stella (aunt), 29
Stiefel, Arnold, 174–75
Sunrise Cassette, 74
Super Bowl XXXVII, 192
Swing (show), 102–3, 110, 112. *See
    also Forever Swing* (show)

talent contests, 51, 54, 58. *See also*
    International Youth Talent
    Search; Pacific National
    Exhibition (PNE)
Taylor, Elizabeth, 163
Temple Sholom, 32, 43, 103
Thompson, Linda, 136, 140, 141,
    151, 157, 194
Thompson, Ron, 144
Thrasher, Sibel, 51, 211
Timuss, Debbie
    career, 154
    at Feinstein's, 197

in Las Vegas, 164
Michael Bublé (album), 156
as Michael Bublé's girlfriend,
    67, 95–96, 228–29
move back to Vancouver, 130
move to L.A., 150
Party of the Century, 111
Red Rock Diner, 82
in *Swing* and *Forever Swing,*
    102, 112, 113, 126–27
Tom Whalley party, 186–87
Today Show, The, 193
Tommy Vickers Orchestra, 103
Totally Blonde (film), 131–33
Turtle Productions, 89

University of Montana, 24

van Keken, Martin, 70, 214
Van Slee, Andrew, 131–32
Vancouver Youth Theatre, 60
Vinson, Ridley, 90
Virginia (half-sister), 15–16
Vogue Theatre Restoration Society,
    111

W5, 201–2
Walsh, Mary, 119
Warner Bros., 176–77, 178–81,
    192, 194
Warwick, Dionne, 111
Weston, Hilary and Galen, 121
Whalley, Tom, 176–77, 178, 186
William Morris Agency, 105–6,
    182–83
Winter Garden, 200
Wright, Chuck, 28–29